W9-BXY-327

UNSOLVED

CONSPIRACIES

METRO BOOKS
New York

An Imprint of Sterling Publishing Co., Inc.
1166 Avenue of the Americas
New York, NY 10036

Metro Books and the distinctive Metro Books logo
are registered trademarks of Sterling Publishing Co., Inc.

© 2018 Quarto Publishing plc

All rights reserved. No part of this publication may be reproduced,
stored in a retrieval system, or transmitted in any form or by any means
(including electronic, mechanical, photocopying, recording, or otherwise)
without prior written permission from the publisher.

ISBN 978-1-4351-6660-8

For information about custom editions, special sales, and premium and
corporate purchases, please contact Sterling Special Sales at 800-805-5489
or specialsales@sterlingpublishing.com.

Manufactured in China

4 6 8 10 9 7 5 3

www.sterlingpublishing.com

Credits: Design and illustration by Mike Lebihan

UNSOLVED

CONSPIRACIES

PLOTS AND DECEPTIONS THAT HAVE PUZZLED THE GREATEST MINDS

BILL PRICE

METRO BOOKS
New York

CONTENTS

POLITICAL CONSPIRACIES   136

ESPIONAGE AND COVERT OPERATIONS   176

INTRODUCTION

Throughout the course of history, unscrupulous people have conspired together in secret to achieve their nefarious aims. Some of these conspiracies have been discovered and the perpetrators identified, while in other cases the conspiracy has remained undetected, allowing those who took part to get away with it. In *Unsolved Conspiracies*, we examine the middle ground, the gray area between success and failure within which, however convinced we may be that a conspiracy has taken place, it has proved impossible to say for certain exactly what happened or who was involved.

We begin our survey of unsolved conspiracies 3,500 years ago in ancient Egypt, by discussing whether the pharaoh Tutankhamun was murdered as part of a plot to remove him from the throne and install one of his senior advisors in his place. And we bring the book to an end with the killing of Osama bin Laden in 2011 by U.S. Special Forces. After a ten-year manhunt, bin Laden was finally traced to Pakistan, and we examine the extent to which Pakistani intelligence

agencies had known of his whereabouts before he was finally found by the United States. In between, we take a look at a catalog of cover-ups, covert operations, and clandestine dealings which remain shrouded in mystery despite extensive efforts to uncover the truth.

In an effort to impose a degree of order on the conspiracies covered here, the book has been divided up into five categories. In *Suspicious Deaths*, we explore the unanswered questions surrounding some mysterious demises and ask whether foul play could have been at work. As well as Tutankhamun, we examine the circumstances surrounding the Mayerling Incident, the apparent suicide of Crown Prince Rudolf of Austria and his seventeen-year-old mistress, and discuss whether the assassination of John F. Kennedy was really committed by a lone gunman or if, as many people believe, others were involved. Then we move on to *False Flag Operations*. In this chapter we look at what some regard as attempts by a state to provoke war by committing an outrage against its own people through covert means, and then

Left: Jesus blessing Mary Magdalene. Has the Church been concealing the true nature of their relationship for the past two thousand years?

Jesus for two thousand years and if NASA really did land men on the moon, before taking on potential *Political Conspiracies*, such as the possibility that a group of Wall Street bankers attempted to stage a coup d'état against President Franklin D. Roosevelt. We bring the book to a close with *Espionage and Covert Operations*, including a possible attempt by Nazi agents to kidnap the Duke of Windsor during the Second World War so that he could be installed as the puppet leader of the United Kingdom in the event of a successful German invasion.

responding to the event as if it was an enemy attack. We consider, for instance, if the explosion which sank the USS *Maine* was perpetrated by the United States as a means of starting the Spanish–American War, and if Russian secret service agents planted bombs in apartment blocks in Russian cities to provide Vladimir Putin with the provocation he needed to go to war in Chechnya.

In *Cover-Ups*, we discuss such questions as whether the Christian Church has been guarding a secret about the personal life of

Many of the incidents covered in the book have been the subject of convoluted, sometimes bizarre, conspiracy theories, while, in other cases, there can be little doubt that a conspiracy has taken place—even if it is not clear exactly what it entailed. Taken together, a portrait emerges of the tangled webs of lies and deceit that have been spun by those among us who have been prepared to go to almost any lengths to get what they want. We may never be able to fully unravel some of these conspiracies, but we can at least shine some light into places which some people would prefer remained in the dark.

SUSPICIOUS DEATHS

In any investigation of a suspicious death, one of the principal starting points is summed up by the Latin phrase *cui bono?*—literally, "who benefits?"—because whoever has the most to gain has the best motive to commit the crime. In this section, we examine a number of deaths in which it is possible to identify people who have benefited, but who are not actually known for certain to have been the culprits. The death of Alexander the Great, for instance, could have been due to natural causes; alternatively, he might have been poisoned by soldiers in his army who had become disillusioned with his constant wars of conquest and could only envisage going home once he was dead.

Left: Lee Harvey Oswald in his backyard holding the Carcano rifle used to assassinate Kennedy.

This section also covers a number of well-known assassinations in which murder certainly occurred, but doubts exist over exactly who was involved. According to the official investigation, Lee Harvey Oswald acted alone to kill President John F. Kennedy, a conclusion that many people do not accept, alleging instead that a conspiracy of one sort or another must have occurred. Over the years, numerous theories have been put forward, pointing the finger at the United States government, the CIA, the Mafia, the Cubans, and a whole range of others, without solid evidence emerging to prove the involvement of any of them. Every aspect of the assassination has been disputed so that, now, the situation is so confused it is hard to imagine how a satisfactory resolution will ever be achieved.

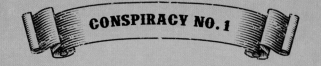
WAS TUTANKHAMUN ASSASSINATED BY HIS SUCCESSOR?

Date: ca. 1323 BCE
Location: Ancient Egypt

Just a teenager when he died, Tutankhamun was immediately succeeded as pharaoh by Ay, his closest adviser. Could the boy king's trusted servant have brought about his premature demise?

The discovery in 1922 of Tutankhamun's tomb, in Egypt's Valley of the Kings, by the British archaeologist Howard Carter, propelled what had been one of the most obscure of all Egyptian pharaohs into the limelight. The spectacular finds made inside the tomb have been seen by millions of people in exhibitions around the world, helping to fuel public interest in all things ancient Egyptian. An X-ray of Tutankhamun's mummy carried out in 1968 revealed a dark patch on the back of his skull and bone fragments in his cranium. This was interpreted as evidence that he had been killed by a blow to the head with a heavy object, leading to speculation that he had been murdered. In any homicide investigation, the main suspects are those people who benefited from the death of the victim and, in the case of Tutankhamun, the person who gained the most was undoubtedly Ay.

Right: Howard Carter with one of his assistants examining Tutankhamun's mummy in its solid gold sarcophagus. Does the mummy hold the secret to the boy king's death?

THE BOY PHARAOH

Tutankhamun ascended to the Egyptian throne during one of the most turbulent periods in the history of ancient Egypt. His father, the pharaoh Akhenaten, had initiated fundamental religious reforms, overturning centuries of tradition by replacing Amun, the principle deity in the Egyptian pantheon of gods, with Aten, who had previously been a relatively minor god. Akhenaten also moved the capital city away from Thebes, the center of the worship of Amun, to the newly built city of Amara. By doing this, he sidelined the previously powerful priesthood of Amun, thereby concentrating religious and political power in his own hands. The exact sequence of succession between Akhenaten's death and Tutankhamun becoming pharaoh is not entirely clear, but around 1332 BCE, at the age of about nine, the boy king ascended to the throne. Over the course of his reign, the reforms instituted by Akhenaten were gradually reversed and Amun, and the associated priesthood, returned to prominence. Ay had held an important position in Akhenaten's court and, though the exact details are not known, appears to have become the power behind the throne when Tutankhamun became pharaoh at such a young age, perhaps even acting as regent until the boy pharaoh was old enough to rule in his own right. It may be coincidental, but Tutankhamun died at the age of about 19, just as he had reached adulthood, so it is not hard to construct a scenario in which Ay either killed Tutankhamun himself or had him killed, in order to retain the position of power he had occupied for the previous ten years.

Ay may have been related to the royal family through marriage, but was not of royal blood himself. In the strictly hierarchical society of ancient Egypt, this must have presented a serious obstacle to his succession. He also does not appear to have been Tutankhamun's designated heir in the event of him dying without issue; this role was filled by Horemheb, the commander of the army. When Tutankhamun's tomb was discovered, the mummified bodies of two stillborn girls were also found inside, and these have been shown by DNA analysis to be his daughters, presumably with his wife and half-sister Ankhesenamun, though there is no evidence of any surviving children.

After Tutankhamun died, then, Horemheb should have gained the throne but appears to have been outmaneuvered by Ay. Unfortunately, very little information survives from the period to help us understand what happened—later pharaohs attempted to erase from history everything relating to Akhenaten, including the reigns of Tutankhamun and Ay, because the reforms he had instituted were regarded as heretical. The resulting gaps in our knowledge mean that we can only now speculate based on what has survived, such as the few clues contained within Tutankhamun's tomb.

Below: Amun, who was reinstated as Egypt's principal deity during Tutankhamun's reign after the Atenist heresy of Akhenaten.

Above: Like many of the grave goods found in Tutankhamun's tomb, the golden funerary mask may have been intended for somebody else.

This gives the impression of being hurriedly prepared, because many of the grave goods, including the sarcophagus and funerary mask, were not originally intended for Tutankhamun, suggesting that his death was unexpected. From the wall paintings within the tomb we also know that Ay officiated at the funeral while Horemheb appears to have been absent. As commander of the army, he could have been away fighting one of the numerous wars against neighboring states that Egypt was almost continually engaged in, and perhaps Ay made use of his absence at the moment of Tutankhamun's death to seize the throne. If this was the case, then Ay could not possibly have acted alone. This would indicate that a conspiracy must have taken place within the Egyptian court: a conspiracy aimed at placing Ay on the throne rather than Horemheb and even, perhaps, getting rid of Tutankhamun at an opportune moment.

RECENT RESEARCH

More recent research carried out on Tutankhamun's mummy, including a CT scan and DNA tests, has shed further light on how he died. The dark spot on the back of his head was actually caused by the resins used by the embalmers who mummified his body, rather than a blow with a heavy object, and the bone fragments in the cranium were also probably dislodged during the embalming process, which involved the removal of his brain. The tests also revealed that Tutankhamun had been suffering from a wide range of health problems at the time of his death, some of which were serious enough to have contributed to it. These included a number of congenital conditions, such as a deformed foot, a cleft palate, and scoliosis, a condition causing an abnormal curvature of the spine. He had

Above: A depiction of Ay from the Amarna period (ca. 1353–36 BCE). Almost all references to Ay were destroyed after Horemheb succeeded him as pharaoh.

also contracted malaria, including the most severe form of the disease, on a number of occasions.

The scans also showed that, shortly before his death, Tutankhamun had suffered a compound fracture of his left leg and the wound had become infected. This is now thought to be the immediate cause of his death. The range of debilitating diseases he had suffered over the course of his short life may also have contributed, leaving him in a weakened state so that he was not able to recover. The circumstances leading to the broken leg remain unknown and, tempting as it may be to point a finger at Ay, the truth is that we are unlikely ever to know for certain. Whatever the case, Ay ruled for only four years before dying and being succeeded by Horemheb. Ay had nominated his son-in-law to become the next pharaoh, so it appears that another intrigue may have occurred in the royal court. Perhaps politics was as dirty a business in ancient Egypt as it is today.

― ALTERNATIVE ―
THEORIES

An archive of documents found in the archaeological remains of Hattusha, the former capital of the Hittite Empire, has provided a tantalizing glimpse into the period when Tutankhamun ruled Egypt. The Hittite Empire was the major power to the north of Egypt, and one of the Hattusha documents provides details of a letter written by an Egyptian queen to the Hittite king Suppiluliuma I. In it she tells him that her husband has recently died and she has no son. She asks Suppiluliuma to send one of his sons to Egypt to become her husband because she is afraid of what will happen to her. Suppiluliuma sends Zannanza, one of his many sons, in the expectation that he will marry the queen and become pharaoh, but Zannanza dies in unknown circumstances while traveling. The Hittite king writes to Egypt to find out what has happened and is bluntly told by the new pharaoh that his son is dead.

The Egyptian queen and new pharaoh are not identified, but the circumstances described suggest they could have been

Above: A panel from the royal throne depicting Tutankhamun with Ankhesenamun, who appears to have feared for her own life after his death.

Ankhesenamun and Ay. An inscription found on a ring now in the Egyptian Museum in Cairo shows Ankhesenamun and Ay's names linked together, which archaeologists interpret as indicating that they were married. Perhaps Ay married Ankhesenamun after killing her husband to give legitimacy to his claim to the throne. Nothing more is known about how Zannanza died, though it is hard to imagine that Ay, having maneuvered himself into position to become pharaoh, would allow the throne to pass to a Hittite prince.

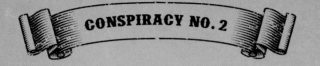

WAS ALEXANDER THE GREAT MURDERED?

Date: ca. 323 BCE
Location: Babylon, ancient Mesopotamia

We don't know exactly how Alexander died, but suspicions have long endured that he was the victim of a murderous plot, perhaps conceived by the very army he commanded.

Alexander is regarded as one of the greatest military commanders ever to have lived. He remained undefeated throughout his career, expanding the territory under his control eastward from Macedonia all the way to northern India, and encompassing the Persian Empire and Egypt. He was considered invincible by the soldiers he commanded, and the strategy and tactics he employed in the numerous campaigns and battles he fought are still studied in military academies today.

ALEXANDER'S ARMY

In 336 BCE, at the age of twenty, Alexander succeeded to the Macedonian throne following the death of his father, Philip of Macedon, who had been assassinated by one of his bodyguards. Some historians have speculated that Alexander was involved in the assassination, though this is solely based on him being the main beneficiary of Philip's death, rather than any actual evidence.

Philip had begun expanding Macedonian territory, gaining control of much of Greece, and Alexander consolidated these gains before embarking on an expedition to the east. The following decade was a period of almost continuous conquest.

Above: A painting by Charles Lebrun depicting the victorious Alexander (in blue) after the Battle of the Hydaspes in what is now Pakistan.

By 326 BCE, Alexander and his army had almost reached the banks of the River Ganges in northern India, having fought their way through what is now Afghanistan and Pakistan. The fighting had been fierce and Alexander had been wounded on a number of occasions, but nevertheless wanted to continue eastward to cross the Ganges. His army refused, mutinying at the prospect of crossing the river, which would take them even further from home.

The mutiny forced Alexander to turn back, and in the following year he arrived in the city of Babylon, on the banks of the River Euphrates in modern-day Iraq, which it appears he intended to make the capital of his empire. By this time, he had already begun to integrate Persian soldiers into the Macedonian army and had married Roxana, a Persian princess. After he arrived in Babylon, he took two more Persian wives as well as presiding over the arranged marriages of a large number of his soldiers to Persian women. He began to wear Persian dress and adopted a number of Persian customs. It must have become increasingly clear to the soldiers who had mutinied in India that Alexander had little intention of ever returning to Macedonia and, in 323 BCE, their suspicions would have been compounded when he began to plan a campaign to invade the Arabian Peninsula.

THE DEATH OF AN EMPEROR

Before he contracted the illness that would kill him, a number of plots to assassinate Alexander had already been uncovered, so it is reasonable to question the circumstances of his death. Unfortunately, no contemporary account survives, so we can only rely on such later sources as Plutarch, who was writing more than three centuries after the event. From what can be gathered, it appears that Alexander fell ill with a fever after drinking heavily. His condition deteriorated over the course of the following ten days to such an extent that he could no longer speak, and on June 10, 323 BCE, at the age of just thirty-two, he died.

It is impossible to be certain what caused Alexander's death. One line of speculation suggests that he died of typhoid or a severe form of malaria, while a different theory alleges that years of heavy drinking combined with the cumulative effects of the wounds he had received in battle had weakened him so much that he succumbed to a less serious disease, such as influenza. Another possibility is that he was poisoned, perhaps involving a conspiracy among those soldiers who had mutinied in India and given up hope of ever returning home while Alexander remained alive.

An alternative potential conspiracy centers on Antipater, who had governed Macedonia in Alexander's absence and had been removed from his position and summoned to Babylon shortly before Alexander died. This could have been regarded as a death sentence and, as one of Antipater's sons is identified by some sources as Alexander's wine bearer, perhaps Antipater and his son conspired to poison the emperor's wine before such a sentence

— ALTERNATIVE —
THEORIES

Most historians think that Alexander was not assassinated, because the poisons available at that time would have caused his sudden death, rather than a fever followed by a slow deterioration over the course of several weeks. One exception is white hellebore, a plant with highly toxic roots and seeds which is native to Greece and western Asia. It was known to Greek and Persian physicians as an emetic, used in low doses to induce vomiting, but could potentially be fatal, with symptoms similar to those suffered by Alexander. This does not, of course, prove that Alexander died as the result of a conspiracy, but it does show that poisoning cannot be ruled out as the cause of his death either.

Above: The flowers of the white hellebore may look innocent enough, but was this the plant used to poison Alexander the Great?

could be carried out. The only way to establish this for certain would be to examine his remains to test for the presence of any illicit substances. Unfortunately, the location of his tomb is one of the great unsolved mysteries of ancient history, so, short of a remarkable archaeological discovery, it is hard to envisage the truth ever being uncovered.

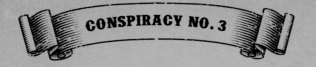

DID CROWN PRINCE RUDOLF OF AUSTRIA REALLY DIE BY SUICIDE?

Date: January 30, 1889
Location: Mayerling, Austria

Crown Prince Rudolf died in a mysterious event that became known as the Mayerling Incident, but it is still not known whether it was a personal tragedy or if there were darker forces at play.

On the morning of January 30, 1889, the bodies of Crown Prince Rudolf, the heir to the throne of the Austro-Hungarian Empire, and Baroness Mary Vetsera, his 17-year-old mistress, were found in a bedroom of an imperial hunting lodge at Mayerling, about 16 miles outside of Vienna. Rudolf, who was thirty years old at the time of his death, was the only son of Emperor Franz Joseph and married to Princess Stephanie of Belgium, with whom he had one daughter. The marriage was not a happy one and Rudolf had previously had affairs with a number of other women. His devoutly Catholic father disapproved of his behavior and forbade him from applying to the Pope for an annulment of the marriage, causing a rift between father and son which, at the time of Rudolf's death, showed no sign of being healed.

A TROUBLED RELATIONSHIP

The personal difficulties between the emperor and heir apparent were only one of many problems besetting the empire. The emperor and his court were obsessed with protocol and social standing, stifling any attempt at reform and modernization at a time of rising nationalism within the ethnically diverse and multilingual empire. In 1867, Franz Joseph had been forced to accept a compromise agreement with Hungary to create the dual monarchy of Austria-Hungary, replacing the old Austrian Empire. Other regions were agitating for a similar degree of autonomy or for full independence, including those regions of the Balkans that fell within the empire. Rudolf, who held more liberal views than his conservative father, recognized the aspirations of those subjects who wanted a greater degree of self-government. This contributed to a number of disagreements between the two men, including a particularly bitter argument shortly before Rudolf died.

Above: This portrait of Crown Prince Rudolf, by Eugen Felix, was painted in the hunting lodge at Mayerling where tragedy would ensue.

The exact circumstances in which Rudolf and Mary met their fate are far from clear. Different accounts were given at the time of how the bodies were found, and no autopsies appear to have taken place. The police investigation was closed down quickly and any conclusions it may have reached were not made public. The most likely explanation is that Rudolf and Mary had entered into a suicide pact, and either the pair had taken their own lives or one had murdered the other and then killed him/herself. The Austrian government then attempted to cover up the details in an effort to limit the damage such a scandal might have caused the monarchy.

MURDER OR SUICIDE?

Very little concern appears to have been shown for Mary Vetsera and her family. Her body was removed from the hunting lodge

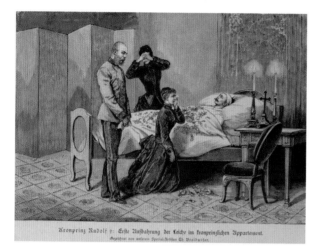

Kronprinz Rudolf †: Erste Aufbahrung der Leiche im kronprinzlichen Appartement.
Gezeichnet von unserem Special-Artisten Th. Breitwieser.

Above: An engraving of Emperor Franz Joseph and Empress Elisabeth at the deathbed of Crown Prince Rudolf, their only son and heir.

in secret and buried almost immediately, then a story was put out that Rudolf had died from sudden heart failure. No mention at all was made of Mary until news began to leak out in foreign newspapers and, once it had become known that she was involved, the story was changed to suggest the couple had taken their own lives in a suicide pact. Conflicting reports in newspapers claiming that the couple had either been poisoned or had died from gunshot wounds caused intense speculation. This was further enhanced by unsubstantiated rumors that the door of the bedroom where they had been found had been locked and a window had been open. This suggested the possibility that Rudolf and Mary had been murdered by an unknown assailant.

No evidence has ever come to light to confirm that Rudolf and Mary were the victims of an assassination, and there were few obvious suspects with a motive to kill the couple. Nationalists from one of the ethnic groups within the Austro-Hungarian Empire could have conspired to kill them, or a faction within the Austrian court who objected to Rudolf's liberal views and lifestyle could have decided he was not fit to succeed his father. In truth, it is impossible to say for certain, and the more likely explanation is that Rudolf, who is reputed to have previously expressed suicidal tendencies, could not continue living the life expected of him and so entered into a suicide pact with Mary.

As Rudolf was the Emperor's only son, the line of succession passed to Franz Joseph's younger brother, Archduke Karl Ludwig, and, when Karl Ludwig died in 1896, to his son, Archduke

ALTERNATIVE THEORIES

In 2015, bank officials opened a leather folder that had been deposited in the vault of a private bank in Vienna in 1926 and left untouched ever since. It was found to contain three letters written by Mary Vetsera in Mayerling shortly before her death. It also contained a number of other documents relating to her, including her birth certificate. The letters were addressed to her mother, brother, and sister, and asked for their forgiveness. In the letter to her mother, she wrote, "I am happier in death than I was in life." If these letters are genuine, then it is reasonable to conclude that Rudolf and Mary really did die by suicide, but, as their provenance before 1926 is not known, they could be forgeries, produced either as part of a cover-up or as a hoax.

Above: Baroness Mary Vetsera was just seventeen when she died alongside the Crown Prince. We still don't know for sure if the pair made a suicide pact.

Franz Ferdinand. As we will see on the following pages, the assassination of Franz Ferdinand would prove to be the spark that ignited the First World War, so it could be argued that an unforeseen consequence of the deaths of Rudolf and Mary, whatever the circumstances, was one of the most devastating wars in human history.

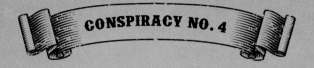

WHO WAS BEHIND THE ASSASSINATION OF ARCHDUKE FRANZ FERDINAND?

Date: June 28, 1914
Location: Sarajevo, Bosnia

The assassination of Franz Ferdinand sparked a chain of events that would change the course of world history, but it is still not known whether his murder was a state-sponsored conspiracy.

The Archduke Franz Ferdinand, the heir apparent to the Austro-Hungarian Empire, was assassinated along with his wife, Sophie, Duchess of Hohenberg, on June 28, 1914, while on a visit to Sarajevo, the capital city of Bosnia. Their killer was Gavrilo Princip, a nineteen-year-old Bosnian Serb. The reason why the deaths of these two people led to the First World War, in which about ten million combatants died, remains the subject of intense debate among historians today. No simple explanation exists, but at the heart of the matter was the Austro-Hungarian belief that Serbia was responsible for the murders.

THE POWDER KEG

By 1914, the great powers of Europe had become divided into two power blocks, with Britain, France, and Russia on one side, and

Germany and Austria-Hungary on the other. Members of the competing blocks had made agreements to the effect that each state would support the other(s) if one was attacked. The pacts offered the potential for a relatively minor incident to escalate into a major conflict if it involved two states from either side of the divide. This was the scenario that played out when Austria-Hungary blamed Serbia for Ferdinand's assassination, because Serbia, though not a major power itself, had long-standing ties to Russia based on shared ethnicity and religion.

Tension between Austria-Hungary and Serbia had been high since 1908, when Austria-Hungary completed the annexation of Bosnia from the Ottoman Empire, having already taken much of the territory into its empire four decades previously. Serbia, which had gained full independence from the Ottoman Empire in 1867, was bound by treaty not to interfere in Bosnia after it had been annexed. But factions within Serbia held expansionist ambitions to form "Greater Serbia," a state that would incorporate all the regions of the Balkans where ethnic Serbs lived.

ASSASSINAT DE L'ARCHIDUC HÉRITIER D'AUTRICHE ET DE LA DUCHESSE SA FEMME A SARAJEVO

Above: A French newspaper illustration depicts the moment Gavrilo Princip assassinated the Archduke and Duchess.

More than 40 percent of the population of Bosnia were Bosnian Serbs, the largest ethnic group in the country. Secret organizations dedicated to creating Greater Serbia had sprung up in Bosnia and Serbia, and one of the methods employed to achieve this aim was to agitate against Austro-Hungarian rule in the country. Gavrilo Princip had joined one of these organizations, known as Young Bosnia, while at school in Sarajevo and, after moving to Belgrade in 1912, he came to the attention of Major Voja Tankosic, an officer in the Serbian secret service. Tankosic was also a member

Left: Gavrilo Princip, in the middle of the front row, at his trial. He was found guilty, but escaped the death penalty because of his young age.

of the Black Hand, another secret society dedicated to Serbian nationalism, led by Dragutin Dimitrijevic, known as Apis, who was the head of Serbian military intelligence. Apis is the key figure to consider when attempting to understand if the conspiracy to assassinate Franz Ferdinand was linked to the Serbian government, because his important position implied that he was closely associated with senior politicians.

In the months leading up to the assassination in 1914, Tankosic provided a group of Young Bosnia members, including Princip, with weapons and training, then smuggled them into Bosnia with the collusion of Serbian border guards. On June 28, six of the group were among the crowds lining the route Franz Ferdinand's car was due to take when he arrived in Sarajevo that morning. As the car passed one of them, he threw a grenade which bounced off the vehicle and exploded next to the car behind, injuring a number of people, though not the Archduke or Duchess. Their car sped off to the reception that had been arranged for them in the city hall, passing Princip, who was further along the route, before he'd had time to react.

Right: An arrest on the day of the assassinations. The man being held on the right could be Gavrilo Princip, though it is not known for certain.

After the reception, the Archduke and Duchess decided to visit the hospital where the people injured in the attack were being treated. Their driver appears to have been unsure of the route and taken a wrong turn. After realizing his mistake he stopped the car, with the apparent intention of reversing or turning round, coming to a halt exactly adjacent to where Princip happened to be standing. Princip seized the opportunity, shooting both the Archduke and Duchess at close range, hitting Sophie in the stomach and Franz Ferdinand in the neck. Sophie was dead before their car reached the hospital and Franz Ferdinand died shortly after it arrived.

FROM CRISIS TO WAR
The authorities in Sarajevo arrested almost all of the gang involved in the attack and from them learned of the role played by Tankosic. The Austro-Hungarians do not appear to have been aware of the involvement of Apis, perhaps because he had not made himself known to any of the gang, but nevertheless came to the conclusion that the Serbian state was behind the assassination. Had the Austro-Hungarians taken some form of punitive action against Serbia immediately, a wider war might have been avoided;

instead, they vacillated for a month while attempting to make up their minds what to do, a period now known as the July Crisis.

Over the course of July, the German government gave its full support to Austria-Hungary no matter what it decided to do, a commitment known as the "blank cheque," while Russia made it clear that it would not allow Serbia to be attacked without retaliation. On July 23, Austria-Hungary finally made its move, issuing Serbia with an ultimatum demanding it take action against any Serbians involved in the assassination. The ultimatum was worded in such a way as to make it impossible for the Serbians to accept in full without compromising their sovereignty and, even though they accepted most of the terms, on July 28, Austria-Hungary launched an invasion. Russia responded by mobilizing its army, prompting Germany to initiate the so-called Schlieffen Plan, which involved mounting a rapid invasion of France through neutral Belgium while fighting a holding war against Russia in the east. Once this plan had been put into action, Britain demanded that Germany withdraw from Belgium and, when this did not happen, declared war. In a matter of a few days, the crisis in the Balkans had escalated into a major European conflict.

No conclusive evidence has ever come to light to show that the Serbian government was involved in the plot to assassinate Franz Ferdinand. The Serbian prime minister, Nikola Pašic, always maintained that he knew nothing about it, while Tankosic died in combat and Apis was executed during the First World War—any knowledge they may have had connecting the conspiracy to the Serbian government died with them. It would appear unlikely that the Black Hand could have operated without influential support. More than a hundred years have now passed and it seems unlikely that we will ever know for sure who was involved in the conspiracy, or whether Austria-Hungary was justified in accusing Serbia of complicity.

— ALTERNATIVE — THEORIES

Of all the European powers involved in the outbreak of the First World War, Russia's role is the least understood. After the Russian Revolution in 1917, there appears to have been little interest within the newly formed Soviet Union in researching the involvement of Tsarist Russia in the events leading up to war. And until the fall of the Soviet Union, Western historians had no access to Russian archives. An indication of possible Russian involvement in the assassination of Franz Ferdinand was provided by Apis in a statement he gave to a Serbian court martial he faced in 1917. He had been indicted on what are now thought to have been false charges concerning a plot to assassinate the Serbian king. During the trial Apis admitted his involvement in the Sarajevo plot and went on to claim that the Russian military attaché to Serbia, Viktor Artamonov, had financed the operation.

Apis was found guilty of treason and executed, while Artamonov declined

Above: Dragutin Dimitrijevic, or Apis, admitted his part in the Sarajevo assassinations without disclosing any Russian involvement.

to comment on any role he may have played in the plot. In an interview given in the late 1920s, he said he was on holiday at the time of Franz Ferdinand's assassination. Other sources within Serbia have suggested that Apis and Artamonov had been in regular contact as the plot unfolded, but, even if this was the case, no definitive evidence directly implicating Artamonov, or the Russian government, has ever come to light.

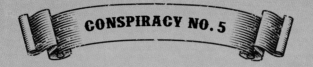
WHAT CAUSED DAG HAMMARSKJÖLD'S PLANE TO CRASH?

Date: September 18, 1961
Location: Ndola, Zambia

An investigation concluded that the plane crash that killed UN Secretary-General Dag Hammarskjöld in 1961 was caused by pilot error, but this verdict has been questioned ever since.

Hammarskjöld had been United Nations (UN) Secretary-General for eight years at the time of his death on September 18, 1961. He was flying from Léopoldville, the capital city of the Republic of the Congo, to Ndola in Northern Rhodesia, now Zambia, to begin ceasefire negotiations with Moise Tshombe, the leader of the breakaway state of Katanga. The Republic of the Congo (now the Democratic Republic of the Congo) had gained independence from Belgium in May 1960 and, in the chaotic aftermath, the mineral-rich southeastern state of Katanga was attempting to secede from the central government. The situation escalated with the involvement of the Soviet Union on the government side and a large contingent of foreign mercenaries fighting for the breakaway state. The UN sent in a peacekeeping force, which had the opposite effect to that intended, as the UN troops became embroiled in the fighting. Hammarskjöld had been due to meet Tshombe in Ndola, just over the border in British-controlled Northern Rhodesia, in an effort to defuse the situation—but, of course, he never got there.

A SUSPICIOUS DEATH

Almost as soon as Hammarskjöld's plane had crashed, killing him and fifteen others, speculation began that Western companies with mining interests in Katanga could have been involved in his death, possibly with the collusion of intelligence services from those countries where the companies were based, which included Britain, Belgium, and the United States. This was based on the premise that Hammarskjöld had advocated a peace deal in the Republic of the Congo which did not involve the secession of Katanga. Moreover, if such a deal could not be negotiated, he had also proposed using UN forces to put down the rebellion.

Above: A portrait of Dag Hammarskjöld taken in 1953, shortly after he was appointed Secretary-General of the United Nations.

The Western powers were concerned about the growing influence of the Soviet Union on the Republic of the Congo's government, and it would emerge decades later that the intelligence services of Britain, Belgium, and the United States had all played a role in deposing Patrice Lumumba, the state's first democratically elected prime minister, who had been executed in January 1961. If the Republic of the Congo regained control of Katanga, the mining concessions granted to Western companies would be in danger of being nationalized, so the Western powers were opposed to the ceasefire plan proposed by Hammarskjöld. This on its own does not necessarily imply that the intelligence services from any of the Western powers were involved in Hammarskjöld's death. However, evidence that has emerged over the years since the plane crash

Above: British investigators inspect the wreckage of the plane at the crash site near Ndola in Northern Rhodesia.

certainly suggests that there was more to it than the initial investigation found.

The plane, a Douglas DC-6, crashed just after midnight, shortly before it was due to land at Ndola. Eyewitness accounts tell of a bright flash in the sky that night and, of seeing uniformed men at the crash site the following morning, several hours before it was officially said to have been found. Several witnesses said they had seen bullet holes in the fuselage of the plane before being ordered to leave the area. Most of these witnesses were either not interviewed during the subsequent investigation or their accounts were ignored. A UN official who went to the crash site and saw Hammarskjöld's body later recounted seeing a hole in his forehead which was not visible on any photographs taken at the scene. It has emerged that the photographs had been altered before being included in the investigation report and, while this does not constitute direct evidence that Hammarskjöld had been shot, it does highlight serious failings in the report.

The UN official who saw the body also reported that Hammarskjöld had earth and grass stains on his hands and clothes, raising the possibility that he had survived for a period after the crash and had crawled out of the wreckage. Two of his security detail had bullet wounds when they were found, which the investigation report stated were caused by bullets from the guns they were carrying exploding in the fire that had engulfed the plane after it crashed. An independent forensics expert later described this possibility as being extremely unlikely. One of the security personnel actually did survive the crash, U.S. Army sergeant Harold Julien. He was taken to a hospital in Ndola where he died from his injuries five days later. Some witnesses reported that, before he died, he had spoken of a series of explosions before the crash, but the investigation discounted these reports. It is also notable that the U.S. government apparently made no effort to move Julien from the hospital in Ndola, which had very basic facilities, to a hospital better equipped to treat the serious injuries he had suffered.

A SECOND PLANE

In 2011, fifty years after the event, details emerged for the first time of intercepted radio transmissions picked up from a pilot flying over Ndola at the time of the crash by an American listening station in Cyprus. According to one of the American officers working for the National Security Agency (NSA) at the listening station, the pilot talked about attacking and shooting down another plane which he identified as a DC-6. If a record of such a radio intercept exists, it has never been released by the NSA to any of the investigations into the crash. A number of witnesses have spoken of hearing another plane in the vicinity of the crash, and the U.S. ambassador to the Republic of the Congo sent a telegram to Washington shortly after the incident to say

Below: A Transair Sweden Douglas DC-6 similar to the plane that crashed, killing Hammarskjöld and fifteen others.

Left: Dag Hammarskjöld in his UN office in 1959. By this time he had antagonized Western governments with his forward-thinking stance on decolonization.

that Hammarskjöld's plane had been shot down by a mercenary pilot from Belgium, though it is not known how the ambassador obtained this information.

An article published in *The Guardian* newspaper in 2014 identified the pilot of the second plane as being Jan van Risseghem, a Belgian military pilot thought to have been flying as a mercenary for the Katangese at the time. Before he died in 2007, Van Risseghem had denied being in Katanga in 1961, but there are a number of eyewitness accounts placing him in the region and indicating that he was flying fighter jets for the Katanga Air Force. This does not mean that he was involved in bringing down Hammarskjöld's plane, but it does provide further credence to the growing body of evidence supporting the theory that the crash was not an accident.

In 2016, Ban Ki-moon, the then UN Secretary-General, ordered a new investigation into the circumstances of his predecessor's death. Even so, unless the NSA releases its classified files relating to the radio intercepts from the night of the crash, the exact cause of the death of Dag Hammarskjöld and the fifteen others who were with him on the plane that night appears likely to remain unknown.

— ALTERNATIVE —
THEORIES

If allegations that Western powers were involved in Dag Hammarskjöld's death are correct, then it is possible that, rather than being killed solely over his stance on Katanga, he was assassinated because of his support for decolonization across the African continent and in general. After becoming United Nations Secretary-General in 1953, Hammarskjöld presided over an organization which was changing rapidly, as many countries joined on gaining independence. At its inception in 1945, there had been fifty-one member states; by the time of Hammarskjöld's death in 1960, that number had doubled. Now, those Western countries who had made up the core of the original membership could no longer rely on having a majority in the UN's general assembly.

Support for decolonization made Hammarskjöld a deeply unpopular figure with the former colonial powers, particularly because he opposed their attempts to maintain control of such assets as mining concessions after their

Above: The United Nations General Assembly hall in New York. The UN was changing rapidly during Hammarskjöld's tenure as Secretary-General.

colonies had become independent, as Belgium tried to do in the Democratic Republic of the Congo. Removing Hammarskjöld from his position as Secretary-General would not have been possible because of the support he enjoyed among the new member states, so a decision could have been taken to assassinate him. As well as getting rid of him, the intention could also have been to send a message to future UN general secretaries of the potential dangers they could face if they continued Hammarskjöld's practice of opposing Western interests.

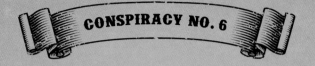

WHO WAS INVOLVED IN THE ASSASSINATION OF JOHN F. KENNEDY?

Date: November 22, 1963
Location: Dallas, Texas, USA

Conspiracy theories abound that President John F. Kennedy may not have been killed by a single gunman acting alone, but by higher powers that wanted him gone—permanently.

A week after the assassination, Lyndon B. Johnson, the newly sworn-in president, set up the Warren Commission to investigate the circumstances of Kennedy's death. The findings of the commission were that he had been killed by Lee Harvey Oswald and that Oswald had acted alone. This conclusion was not accepted by everybody, perhaps because many did not want to believe that such a momentous event could have been perpetrated by a single man. The nature of the evidence pointing toward a lone gunman came under intense scrutiny and questions have been raised ever since over almost every detail of the shooting.

OSWALD

President Kennedy was assassinated at about 12:30 p.m. on November 22, 1963, in Dallas, Texas. He was traveling in an open-topped limousine and was passing through Dealey Plaza when the bullets that killed him were fired. He was hit twice, once in the upper back and again in the head, while a third shot appears to have missed the target. The noise of the shots was initially taken by many people in the vicinity to be either firecrackers or the sound of a car backfiring and, as the sound echoed off the surrounding buildings, it was not immediately apparent to everybody present where exactly the noise had come from.

Above: President Kennedy is driven through Dallas in his limousine a few minutes before the assassination. Governor John Connally is sitting in front of him.

A number of witnesses lining the street to watch the presidential motorcade had seen a man fire a rifle from a sixth-floor corner window of the Texas School Book Depository building on the corner of Dealey Plaza and Elm Street. They provided the police with a description, which was circulated to all officers in Dallas, and the book depository was sealed off. Lee Harvey Oswald, who had been seen in the building not long before the shooting, was the only employee who had been at work that day who could not be accounted for afterwards, and his description matched that given by the witnesses.

About seventy minutes after the shooting, Officer J. D. Tippit saw a man matching the description walking along a street about 3 miles from Dealey Plaza. When Tippit approached the man, he was shot four times with a handgun and died from his injuries. Witnesses saw the gunman go into a nearby movie theater, where he was arrested shortly afterwards—it was Oswald. He was initially charged with the murder of Officer Tippit before also being

Above: Jack Ruby, with his back to the camera, shooting Lee Harvey Oswald as he is moved from the Dallas city jail.

charged with the assassination of President Kennedy.

Two days after Oswald had been arrested, he was shot and killed as he was being taken out of the Dallas city jail to be transported to the county jail. His assailant was Jack Ruby, a Dallas nightclub owner with known Mafia connections, who claimed to have shot Oswald to spare Jackie Kennedy the trauma of having to attend the trial of her husband's murderer. Before he had been killed, Oswald had denied any involvement in the assassination and claimed he was a patsy, set up by those who had really assassinated Kennedy. The evidence against him appeared to be strong, but, as his death meant he could not be charged with the murder, the evidence would not be tested in court. With no possibility of a trial, President Johnson set up the Warren Commission to investigate the circumstances surrounding the assassination.

One of the most powerful pieces of evidence against Oswald was the rifle used by the shooter in the book depository. It was found between some boxes on the sixth floor not far from the corner window and was shown to be the same Italian-made Carcano rifle with telescopic sight that Oswald had bought by mail order nine months earlier. Photographs were found among his possessions showing him holding the same rifle, and it was ballistically matched to bullet fragments recovered from the scene of the shooting. It was also matched to a bullet found on the stretcher used to carry John Connally, the Governor of Texas, to hospital. Connally had been sitting in front of Kennedy in the presidential limousine and had been injured by one of the same bullets that had hit the president. On the morning of the assassination, Oswald had arrived at work carrying a long, thin package, which he had said contained curtain rods for his house. If Oswald really was a patsy, then somebody had done a very thorough job of stitching him up.

Investigations into Oswald's life before the shooting brought up a mass of contradictory details which served only to confuse the matter. At the age of seventeen he had joined the U.S. Marines, where, as a routine part of training, he had been taught to shoot a rifle and had achieved the grade of sharpshooter. In October 1959, a month after leaving the Marines, he defected to the Soviet Union. He lived there for almost three years before being repatriated to the United States, bringing his Russian wife with him and living at a number of addresses in Fort Worth, Dallas, and New Orleans. He became involved with several different organizations which either supported or opposed the revolutionary government of Fidel Castro in Cuba and, in September 1963, he traveled to Mexico City, where he visited the Cuban embassy to apply for a travel visa, saying he wanted to go from Cuba back to the Soviet Union. His application was refused and he returned to Dallas, where, five weeks before the shooting, he found a job in the book depository.

Right: Mugshot of Lee Harvey Oswald taken after his arrest for the murder of Officer Tippett. Oswald was later charged with the Kennedy assassination.

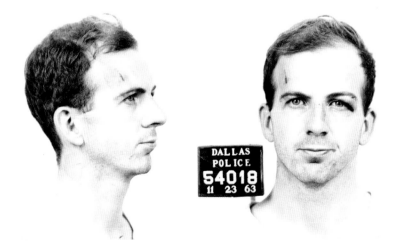

Left: A Dallas police officer shows reporters the Carcano rifle found on the sixth floor of the Texas Book Depository.

THE CIA AND THE MAFIA

Oswald's bizarre life could hardly have failed to attract the attention of the security services. On his return from Mexico City, the FBI attempted to interview him, but failed to find him and instead talked to his wife. As a former defector who had returned to the United States from the Soviet Union, Oswald must surely have been known to the CIA, too. The CIA's subsequent lack of cooperation with the investigations into the assassination, and the agency's refusal to release classified files relating to it, has fueled speculation of, at the very least, a cover-up, if not direct CIA involvement in the shooting. One of the most commonly repeated conspiracy theories is that rogue elements from the CIA colluded with the Mafia to get rid of a president who they considered had betrayed them, not only over U.S. policy toward Cuba, but also because it is alleged that the Mafia had played a role in getting Kennedy elected as president. After winning the election, he appointed his brother Robert Kennedy to the position of attorney general in his administration, and Robert then began an aggressive campaign against organized crime in the United States. Before the Cuban Revolution in 1959, American businesses owned significant holdings in the country, and the Mafia were involved in running a number of highly profitable casinos. On becoming president, Castro began a program of nationalizing businesses and seizing foreign-held assets, including those of the Mafia. He also expelled all known Mafia members in Cuba, a move that is estimated to have cost them hundreds of millions of dollars in lost assets and future profits. This led to CIA operatives and members of the Mafia working together on numerous unsuccessful assassination attempts on Castro, and to an invasion of Cuba by CIA-trained and funded Cuban exiles. This operation became known as the Bay of Pigs, after the stretch of the Cuban coastline where it occurred. The invasion was a complete failure and some of the CIA operatives involved blamed Kennedy, who had authorized it but had then refused to allow the use of sufficient U.S. military support to ensure its success.

No undisputed evidence has ever come to light directly linking either the CIA or the Mafia to the assassination and, in truth, there is nothing concrete to suggest a conspiracy of any sort occurred.

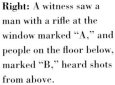

Right: A witness saw a man with a rifle at the window marked "A," and people on the floor below, marked "B," heard shots from above.

Perhaps the most compelling single piece of evidence pointing toward a conspiracy is the film footage known as the Zapruder film. It was shot in Dealey Plaza by Abraham Zapruder, who was standing on a concrete bollard next to a grass bank—the now famous grassy knoll—and filmed Kennedy's motorcade as it went past. The film shows in graphic detail the moment when Kennedy was shot in the head. A gaping wound can clearly be seen in his forehead and his body slumps backward and to the left, giving the impression that the bullet had come from the direction of the grassy knoll, to his front and right, rather than from the School Book Depository, which was behind him. If a second shooter was involved, perhaps firing from behind the wooden fence running along the top of the grassy knoll, then there could be no doubt that a conspiracy had occurred, though we would still not know who was implicated. A number of witnesses reported seeing men in the car park behind the wooden fence at the time of the assassination, but nobody actually saw a rifle or anybody shooting from that position.

Many people—according to opinion polls, more than 60 percent of Americans—believe that others besides Oswald were involved in Kennedy's assassination, but the evidence as it stands today cannot be used to confirm such suspicions. More than fifty years after one of the defining events of the twentieth century, it is hard to envisage a complete resolution ever emerging, unless the classified CIA files, should they ever be released, contain revelatory new material. It is also possible that no conspiracy took place and Lee Harvey Oswald really did act alone. If that is the case, any chance of discovering his motives for killing Kennedy, whatever they may have been, died with him.

─ ALTERNATIVE ─
THEORIES

Most of the conspiracy theories concerning the Kennedy assassination concentrate on American organizations and individuals, particularly the CIA and the Mafia. Grander schemes suggest that it could have been a coup staged by Lyndon Johnson or that it was directed by the military–industrial complex, a supposed alliance between the U.S. military, arms manufacturers, politicians, and prominent businessmen. The principal problem with many of these theories is that they would have involved a huge number of people. It is hard to believe that such a plot could possibly have been kept secret at the time and that nobody would have spoken of it since.

An entirely different theory suggests that the assassination had little or nothing to do with Americans, but was instead carried out by the Cuban secret service on the orders of Fidel Castro. The CIA had attempted to kill Castro many times, and this theory suggests that the Cubans killed Kennedy in retaliation. One version

Above: The Cuban leader Fidel Castro, always denied that Cuba had played any role in the assassination of President Kennedy.

envisages Oswald being recruited by the Cubans as an assassin, while another claims that he was a patsy used by those Cuban agents who had really carried out the assassination. Castro always denied this, saying that it would have been crazy because, had Cuban involvement been discovered, it would have given the United States the grounds it needed to mount a full-scale invasion of Cuba.

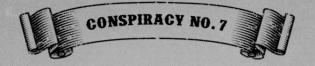
WAS PRINCESS DIANA'S DEATH AN ACCIDENT OR WAS SHE MURDERED?

Date: August 31, 1997
Location: Paris, France

Most people accept that Princess Diana's death was a tragic accident. A small number, though, are vehement in their belief that members of the British establishment conspired to kill her.

Diana had been the subject of intense media interest ever since her engagement to Prince Charles in 1981, when she was nineteen years old. The marriage had not been a happy one; both Charles and Diana had been involved with other people before they separated, and in 1996 they divorced. In July 1997, Diana began a relationship with Dodi Fayed, the forty-two-year-old son of the Egyptian businessman Mohamed Al-Fayed, who, among many other interests, owned the Ritz Hotel in Paris and Harrods department store in London. A media frenzy began as rumors circulated that Diana and Dodi were about to get engaged and on August 30, 1997, the world's paparazzi assembled outside the Ritz in Paris to capture the couple's arrival after a short holiday in the Mediterranean on Fayed's yacht.

Right: The wreckage of Diana's limousine being removed from the Place de l'Alma tunnel where it crashed.

AN ACCIDENT IN PARIS

Shortly after midnight, Diana and Dodi left the Ritz by a back entrance, heading for an apartment in Paris owned by Mohamed Al-Fayed. They were traveling in a black Mercedes limousine driven by Henri Paul, the deputy head of security at the hotel, and were accompanied by Trevor Rees-Jones, one of Mohamed Al-Fayed's security team, who was sitting in the front passenger seat. Some members of the press had been waiting at the hotel's back entrance, and they pursued Diana and Dodi's black Mercedes in a number of cars and by motorbike. The limo was traveling at considerable speed, presumably in an effort to lose the paparazzi, when Paul apparently lost control of the car as it was entering the Place de l'Alma tunnel. It swerved across the road and crashed head-on into a concrete pillar at a speed later estimated to have been 65 mph. It then spun around and careered backward into the wall of the tunnel.

Dodi Fayed and Henri Paul were pronounced dead at the scene, while Diana and Trevor Rees-Jones both survived the initial crash. They had sustained serious injuries and were taken to a nearby hospital. Rees-Jones survived, but Diana had major internal injuries and died later that night. The media initially reported that the pursuing press cars and bikes had been responsible for the accident.

Above: A memorial to Princess Diana and Dodi Fayed displayed in Harrods, the London department store formerly owned by Dodi's father, Mohamed Al-Fayed.

An inquiry later established that the press vehicles had been too far away from the Mercedes at the time of the crash to have caused it, but that the car had been traveling at such speed in an attempt to lose them. Henri Paul was found to have alcohol and prescription medicines in his bloodstream, which could have impaired his driving ability and judgment, leading to the conclusion that his reckless driving had been the primary cause of the accident. The inquiry also noted that none of the occupants of the car had been wearing seat belts and that this was a contributory factor to the three deaths.

ACCIDENT OR ROYAL CONSPIRACY?

Traces of white paint found on the Mercedes after the crash were thought to have come from a Fiat Uno seen in the tunnel by a number of witnesses, leading to claims that the crash may not have been caused by driver error alone. Despite an intensive effort by the French police to find the white Fiat, it has never been found and the driver has not come forward, fueling speculation that there was a conspiracy to kill Diana. The most vocal proponent of this view has been Mohamed Al-Fayed, who has stated on many occasions that he believes the British secret service MI6 were involved, and that they had acted on the orders of Prince Philip, the Duke of Edinburgh.

Al-Fayed claimed not only that Diana was planning on getting engaged to his son and that she was pregnant with his child at the time of her death, but that Henri Paul had been involved with MI6. The prospect of Diana marrying an Egyptian Muslim had, he said, caused the British royal family severe embarrassment, enough for

— ALTERNATIVE —
THEORIES

At the 2013 trial of Danny Nightingale, a British SAS soldier accused of possessing an illegal firearm, allegations surfaced from another SAS soldier, known only as Soldier N, that members of the regiment had been involved in Diana's death. These allegations received extensive coverage in the media and rekindled claims of a conspiracy to kill Diana. After the initial burst of publicity had died down, it emerged that the allegations had actually been made by Soldier N's estranged wife (whose identity was kept a secret). She claimed her husband had told her that the SAS had killed

Above: Danny Nightingale and his wife, Sally. Allegations of SAS involvement in Diana's death were made at Nightingale's trial for the possession of a firearm.

Diana and she had then passed the information to the police, who had not considered it to be credible.

them to want to get rid of her. In 2004, a British police inquiry began to re-examine the evidence and investigate the claims of a conspiracy. After two years, a report was published which stated that no evidence of a conspiracy had been found and that Diana had not been pregnant. It came to the same conclusion as the original French inquiry: that Diana's death was the result of an accident and that Paul had been primarily responsible for the crash. But in the absence of such a key piece of information—the identity of the person who was driving the white Fiat Uno—some doubt must still remain over the exact circumstances of her death.

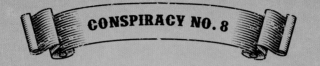

DID DR. DAVID KELLY REALLY DIE BY SUICIDE?

Date: July 17, 2003
Location: Harrowdown Hill, Oxfordshire, UK

The death of the British government weapons inspector Dr. David Kelly was attributed to suicide, but questions about the murky circumstances surrounding his demise have been asked ever since.

D r. Kelly was a leading authority on biological weapons who had been employed by the British Ministry of Defence and the United Nations (UN) as a weapons inspector. He visited Iraq on numerous occasions after the end of the first Gulf War in 1991 to investigate whether the Iraqi regime of Saddam Hussein possessed weapons of mass destruction (WMDs) in defiance of UN resolutions which had ordered all such weapons to be destroyed. The regime's persistent obstruction of the weapons inspectors' work over the course of the next seven years led to the threat of UN-backed military action against Iraq, particularly by the coalition of countries that had invaded Afghanistan in 2001, in the aftermath of 9/11 (see page 84).

THE 45-MINUTE CLAIM

By 2002, and with Saddam allowing weapons inspections to continue, it had become clear that a specific UN resolution

authorizing an invasion of Iraq was highly
unlikely because Russia and France, both
permanent members of the UN Security
Council, announced that they would veto
such a proposal. The United States and
Britain attempted to present a case in
which an invasion would not require a UN
resolution, basing this on the proposition
that Saddam had WMDs which could
be deployed with immediate effect. In
order to back up this assertion, the British
government produced what has become
known as the "September dossier," which
presented intelligence gathered as evidence
for WMDs in Iraq.

Dr. Kelly advised the compilers of the
September dossier, but was subsequently
unconvinced by some of the material it contained, particularly
the claim that Iraq could deploy the WMDs it was alleged to
possess within 45 minutes. This claim had been presented as
demonstrating a threat to British security, and in March 2003
it was cited as justification for the Iraq War, which began
that month. In May, Kelly spoke to Andrew Gilligan, a BBC
journalist, who reported on TV that the 45-minute claim had
been inserted in the dossier by the government, rather than
being based on intelligence. He identified British Prime Minister
Tony Blair's director of communications, Alastair Campbell, as
being responsible for its inclusion. Gilligan described the dossier
as being "sexed up," the intelligence it contained having been
enhanced to provide the necessary justification for war. Gilligan's
implication was clear enough: Tony Blair had taken Britain to
war on the basis of intelligence he knew to be false. If correct,
then Blair had lied to the British Parliament when he presented
the dossier to the House of Commons. By initiating a war without

Above: Dr. David Kelly
was identified by the
Ministry of Defence as
the source of a BBC
report criticizing the
British government.

Above: A U.S. Army checkpoint in Iraq. The rationale for the invasion of Iraq has been heavily criticized.

a UN resolution authorizing military action, he could also potentially be accused of committing a war crime.

A political storm developed after Gilligan's report was broadcast and, unintentionally or otherwise, enough details of his source were revealed by the Ministry of Defence for the press to identify Kelly. He was in a difficult position because, as an employee of the Ministry of Defence, he should have sought clearance before speaking to Gilligan in the first place. In his defense, he claimed that he had not provided Gilligan with any information which had refuted the 45-minute claim, saying that this must have come from another source. It was at this point, in July 2003, that Kelly was called to appear before a government committee investigating the BBC report. Here he was asked to explain his actions and faced an aggressive line of questioning from some of the MPs on the committee.

AN UNLIKELY SUICIDE?

Dr. Kelly was reported missing by his wife at about midnight on July 17, 2003, two days after he had been questioned by the committee, when he failed to return from an afternoon walk in the Oxfordshire countryside. His body was found the following morning at Harrowdown Hill, a wooded area not far from his house. His left wrist had been cut and in his possession were found empty packets of co-proxamol painkillers; it was clear that he had taken twenty-nine tablets. Following a postmortem, the Oxfordshire coroner reached a verdict of suicide. Two weeks later, an inquiry chaired by the judge Lord Hutton began to examine the circumstances surrounding Dr. Kelly's death.

The Hutton inquiry reported its findings in January 2004. It exonerated the government, finding that the September dossier had not been sexed up, and was also highly critical of the BBC's editorial process and management, leading to the resignation of several journalists, including Gilligan, and Greg Dyke, its director-general. These findings attracted widespread criticism among the press, who accused Hutton of presiding over a whitewash aimed solely at protecting the government rather than finding out the truth.

Rather than bringing the matter to a close, the Hutton report only served to increase the number of conspiracy theories surrounding Dr. Kelly's death, and suspicions of a cover-up have persisted. One of the principal unanswered questions concerns the role played in the affair by British security services, in particular MI5, the UK's domestic security agency, and Special Branch, the division of the British police which deals with matters of national security. While the involvement of the security services cannot be considered unusual—after all, Dr. Kelly was a high-profile employee of the Ministry of Defence and had previously worked in Iraq—some of the actions of the agents involved in the investigation have raised questions. They made a thorough search of Dr. Kelly's house, which included stripping the wallpaper from one room, and seized his computers. It has never been made clear why these actions were taken or if the security services were looking for something specific which may have had some bearing on Kelly's death. It is not known what happened to the computers after they were seized and, to date, their location remains a mystery.

Below: The Iraq War led to numerous protests in Britain, with Prime Minister Tony Blair accused of being a liar and a war criminal.

In 2010 a group of nine doctors and forensic scientists collectively questioned the findings of the postmortem, saying that its verdict of suicide was, at the very least, debatable. They argued that the cut in Kelly's wrist would not have led to sufficient blood loss to cause his death, particularly in view of the fact that a relatively small amount of blood was found at the scene. They also observed that cutting the artery in the wrist rarely results in death, and that suicide in a man of fifty-nine—Dr. Kelly's age at the time of his death—is extremely rare. The doctors did not suggest that Dr. Kelly had been murdered, but thought that the proper procedure had not been followed and a full inquest into his death was needed. The paramedics who had first attended Dr. Kelly when he was found went public at this time to say that they had observed only a very small quantity of blood at the scene, adding to the impression that the verdict reached by the original coroner's report, that Kelly had taken his own life, was not entirely consistent with the known facts.

Others have envisaged a scenario in which persons unknown murdered Dr. Kelly to prevent him from making any further damaging revelations concerning the government's conduct in the run-up to the Iraq War. No evidence has been found to implicate any individuals or institutions in his death and, to date, no inquest has been held. It is also worth noting that the intelligence presented in the September dossier has since been found to be wrong. Not only was Saddam Hussein not capable of firing WMDs in 45 minutes, but no usable WMDs have been found in Iraq at all. Despite the obvious failings of the intelligence, a number of the dossier's authors have subsequently been given promotions, while nobody in Britain has been held to account for taking the country into what is now widely perceived to have been an illegal war.

— ALTERNATIVE —
THEORIES

In his book *The Strange Death of David Kelly*, published in 2007, the Liberal Democrat MP Norman Lamb reviewed the available evidence and came to the conclusion that Dr. Kelly had not died by suicide. Lamb noted that Dr. Kelly had told friends that he may be "found dead in the woods," and nobody who knew him, including hiw wife, thought he was likely to kill himself. The nature of the wound on his wrist and the lack of blood at the scene also suggested to Lamb that the official version of his death did not provide an adequate explanation.

After rejecting speculation that the British intelligence services were directly involved, Lamb raised the possibility Dr. Kelly had been murdered by dissident Iraqi groups who had supported the war in Iraq as a means of removing Saddam Hussein from power. According to this theory, these groups hoped to fill the power vacuum left in Iraq after Saddam had been deposed, and the questions raised by Kelly over the justification

Above: U.S. Marines using a tank to pull down a statue of Saddam Hussein in Baghdad after the success of the 2003 invasion of Iraq.

used by the British government to go to war had jeopardized these plans. Lamb went on to suggest that MI6 may have been aware of the Iraqi dissidents' plans and, after Dr. Kelly had been killed, initiated a cover-up to make his murder look like suicide. What Lamb could not provide was incriminating evidence; so, though he makes a plausible case that Dr. Kelly did not die by suicide, his claim of murder by Iraqi dissidents remains an unproven theory.

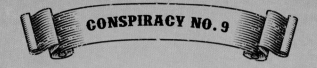

WHO WAS RESPONSIBLE FOR THE POISONING OF ALEXANDER LITVINENKO?

Date: November 23, 2006
Location: London, UK

Shortly before he died, the former Russian spy Alexander Litvinenko accused the Russian president of ordering his assassination, but was there really a connection to the Kremlin?

Litvinenko, a former KGB and FSB operative, had been granted political asylum in Britain in May 2001 after fleeing from prosecution in Russia. Before leaving Russia he had made public allegations that the FSB, the Russian security service that replaced the KGB after the collapse of the Soviet Union, was involved in corruption with the Russian mafia. He had subsequently been removed from his position with the FSB, and Vladimir Putin, then the FSB director, would later say that he had personally sacked Litvinenko. After he had arrived in London, Litvinenko continued to make allegations against the Russian government, claiming the country had become a "mafia state" under Putin, who by that time was President of the Russian Federation.

POISONED BY POLONIUM

On November 1, 2006, Litvinenko became ill and two days later he was taken to Barnet General Hospital and then transferred to University College Hospital in London. After extensive tests, it was determined he had been poisoned by the highly radioactive isotope polonium-210.

Above: After fleeing Russia in 2001, the former FSB agent Alexander Litvinenko became a fierce critic of the Russian president Vladimir Putin.

Polonium-210 is a rare and extremely dangerous substance and almost all of the world's supply is produced in Russia, where it is used in the manufacture of nuclear weapons and in the nuclear power industry. A piece smaller than a grain of salt is extremely likely to be fatal if ingested.

Litvinenko's condition deteriorated over the course of three weeks and, on November 23, he died. Once the nature of his illness had been established, police were able to follow a radioactive trail left by the polonium around London. High levels of radioactivity were found at a hotel where Litvinenko had met three Russians shortly before falling ill, the highest level being traced to a specific teapot. It provided the police with evidence that he had been poisoned by drinking spiked tea.

Two of the Russians at the London meeting were named as Andrei Lugovoy and Dmitry Kovtun, and their movements both before and afterwards were traced through the radioactive trail they had left in the hotel rooms, cars, and airplanes they had used. Litvinenko had only left a radioactive trail after the hotel meeting, demonstrating that his first point of contact with polonium-210 had been at the meeting and not before. By the time this had been established, Lugovoy and Kovtun had returned to Russia. The British authorities attempted to extradite both back to Britain to face murder charges, but the application was refused because the Russian constitution does not permit the extradition of Russian nationals. The third man at the meeting was introduced to Litvinenko as Vladislav Sokolenko. He has never been identified by police and apparently left no radioactive trail.

A RUSSIAN STATE ASSASSINATION?

Lugovoy and Kovtun worked for branches of the Russian security services and, as both left a radioactive trail before the meeting, the police were confident they were the ones who had spiked Litvinenko's tea. Polonium-210 is not an easy substance to obtain and by far the most likely source would be the state-run laboratories in Russia where it is produced. This all adds up to a scenario in which Litvinenko was assassinated by the Russian secret services, but the question of who was ultimately responsible remains unanswered.

The Russian authorities have denied any involvement and Vladimir Putin has said that, in any case, Litvinenko did not know any state secrets, implying that he was not important enough to warrant an assassination. He had defected six years before he was killed and, in London, was being paid by MI6, so, even if he had been in possession of any Russian state secrets, it appears likely that he would already have passed them on. This tends to suggest that however much the Russians may have despised Litvinenko as a traitor, it made little sense to kill him in a way which would so obviously implicate the Russian state.

If we credit the Russian secret services with some intelligence, then it is hard to believe they would not have been aware of the potential diplomatic damage caused by carrying out an assassination in a foreign country. One way in which it would make sense, though, was if, as well as silencing a vocal critic of Vladimir

— ALTERNATIVE —
THEORIES

Litvinenko is reputed to have been in financial difficulty at the time of his death, leading to speculation that, rather than being the subject of a Russian secret service hit, he was involved in an attempt to smuggle polonium-210 out of Russia. The rarity of polonium-210 and its use in nuclear weapons make it highly valuable. In this scenario, Litvinenko was part of a smuggling ring along with Lugovoy and Kovtun and, at some point, had mishandled the polonium-210 and accidentally poisoned himself. What this theory does not take into account is that the highest level of radioactivity was found in the teapot at the hotel where the three of them met, indicating that

Above: The radioactive trail left by polonium-210 led police to a teapot in the London hotel where Litvinenko had met with Lugovoy and Kovtun.

the polonium-210 had not been passed between them but had been put into Litvinenko's tea.

Putin, it was intended to send a message to other Russian defectors and dissidents around the world. Litvinenko's slow and agonizing death would show that, whatever the consequences were for Russia, traitors could expect to face severe retribution for their act of betrayal. It would surely be more than enough to make anybody think twice before criticizing Vladimir Putin, wherever they were in the world or however well protected they thought they were.

FALSE FLAG OPERATIONS

The term "false flag" was originally used in naval warfare to describe a deception operation in which a warship flew the battle flag of an enemy in order to get close to an opposing ship without being recognized. The meaning has broadened to include other spheres of warfare in which disguise has been adopted, and it now most often refers to the staging of an incident that can be blamed on the enemy. The best-known example is the Gleiwitz Incident, in which German soldiers dressed in Polish uniforms attacked a German radio station near the Polish border on September 1, 1939. The attack was then used as justification for the subsequent invasion of Poland.

The details of the Gleiwitz Incident have been firmly established, so it does not feature in this book. Here we consider such unsolved examples as the possibility that the U.S. government carried out the 9/11 terrorist attacks in order to go to war in the Middle East. We also examine variations of the false flag concept, in which one country may have prior knowledge of an enemy attack but does nothing to prevent it, so that it can be used as a reason to declare war. It is alleged, for example, that the United States was aware of the Japanese intention to attack Pearl Harbor. We also consider whether the United States and the United Kingdom could have used fabricated intelligence that the Iraqi regime of Saddam Hussein possessed weapons of mass destruction, in order to provide legitimate grounds for the subsequent invasion of Iraq.

Left: The collapse of the Twin Towers of the World Trade Center in New York during the 9/11 attacks.

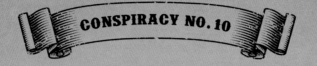

WAS NERO RESPONSIBLE FOR THE GREAT FIRE OF ROME?

Date: July 18, 64 CE
Location: Rome, Italy

Proverbially, the Roman emperor Nero is said to have fiddled while Rome burned. Another theory is that not only did he do nothing, he may have deliberately caused the fire in the first place.

The Great Fire of Rome broke out on the night of July 18, 64 CE, and burned for about six days, destroying a vast area of the city. No contemporary accounts of the event have survived, so we have to rely on the writings of later Roman historians such as Tacitus and Suetonius, both of whom were writing about sixty years after the event. These accounts differ in a number of respects, not least in how the fire started and what Nero was doing at the time.

NERO AND THE CHRISTIANS

According to Tacitus, in the aftermath of the fire Nero blamed the Christian community in Rome for the catastrophe. Tacitus goes on to describe these Christians as scapegoats without actually explaining why they had been targeted or pointing the finger of blame for the fire at Nero, who was identified as the culprit by Suetonius and a number of other writers. If Nero really was responsible, questions still remain over whether he had simply targeted a vulnerable minority to deflect the blame away from himself, or if he had started the fire with the intention of using it as an excuse to begin the persecution of the Christians.

Above: A depiction of people fleeing the flames as fire engulfs Rome, painted in 1785 by the French artist Hubert Robert.

The size of the early Christian community in Rome is not known for certain, but by 57 CE it was large enough for Saint Paul to address one of his epistles to it. Nero had become emperor in 54 CE, succeeding his great-uncle Claudius, and, initially at least, he does not appear to have considered minority groups such as the Christians as presenting any great threat to the Roman Empire. Claudius had banished all Jews from Rome in 49 CE after numerous incidences of social unrest and, on becoming emperor, Nero had allowed the Jews to return. It is not known if the banishment also applied to Christians, who were regarded by some at the time as belonging to a Jewish sect, but, whatever the case, by the time of the fire in 64 CE, it appears that the Christian community in Rome numbered in the thousands and was getting larger.

PERSECUTION

Some modern historians have suggested that early Christians thought Rome was an evil place because they regarded most of its citizens as pagans. Some Christians in the city are thought to have circulated texts to this effect, containing prophecies that the city would be destroyed in a great inferno. If this was the case, then Christians in Rome would have been the obvious target of suspicion in the event of a catastrophic fire breaking out, particularly if it was thought to have been started deliberately.

Tacitus was about nine years old at the time of the fire and may have been in the city, so his account, though written many years later, might have been based on what he had seen for himself and heard from eyewitnesses. He says that the fire began in shops selling what he describes as "flammable goods" near the Circus Maximus, the stadium used for chariot racing, and that it had spread quickly due to a strong wind. Many of the poorer areas of the city were made up of wooden apartment buildings, built close together, so, in the dry weather conditions of summer and fanned by the wind, the fire apparently spread quickly, completely destroying three of Rome's fourteen districts and badly damaging seven more.

Tacitus believed that the fire had spread more widely than could be accounted for by the wind alone, leading him to think that either looters had stoked the fire so they could carry on ransacking, or those who were ordered to set the fire had ensured its spread.

Below: The painting *Nero's Torches*, by the Polish artist Henryk Siemiradzki, depicts Nero persecuting the Christians.

— ALTERNATIVE — THEORIES

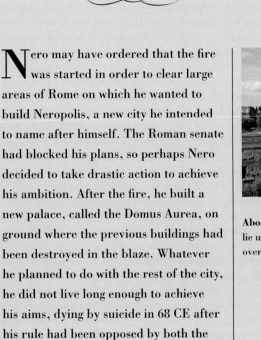

Nero may have ordered that the fire was started in order to clear large areas of Rome on which he wanted to build Neropolis, a new city he intended to name after himself. The Roman senate had blocked his plans, so perhaps Nero decided to take drastic action to achieve his ambition. After the fire, he built a new palace, called the Domus Aurea, on ground where the previous buildings had been destroyed in the blaze. Whatever he planned to do with the rest of the city, he did not live long enough to achieve his aims, dying by suicide in 68 CE after his rule had been opposed by both the senate and the Roman army.

Above: The remains of Nero's Domus Aurea now lie under the Baths of Trajan, which were built over the top of its ruins in 104 CE.

He does not say that Nero gave any such orders, instead writing that the emperor was not in Rome at the time of the fire. This implies that Tacitus did not think Nero responsible for starting the fire; perhaps the emperor simply used it as an excuse to begin persecuting Christians. Whatever the case, hundreds of Christians were killed, by being either thrown to dogs, crucified, or burned alive. It was the beginning of more than two centuries of Roman persecution of Christians, which only officially came to an end in 313 CE, when Emperor Constantine issued the Edict of Milan and legalized Christianity throughout the Roman Empire.

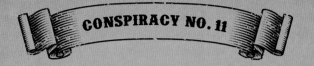
WHO WAS RESPONSIBLE FOR THE SINKING OF THE USS *MAINE?*

Date: February 15, 1898
Location: Havana, Cuba

A huge explosion sunk the USS *Maine* in Havana Harbor on February 15, 1898. What really caused the blast, in which 266 men lost their lives, remains the subject of debate today.

A Spanish mine, sabotage, and a catastrophic accident have all been cited as the source of the explosion, which resulted in the loss of 266 men. Whatever the cause, the sinking of the *Maine* would prove to be the catalyst for the Spanish–American War. This has led to speculation that it was a false flag operation in which the Americans intentionally sank one of their own ships and blamed the Spanish in order to outrage public opinion and justify going to war. The *Maine* had been sent to Cuba three weeks before it sank on what was described as a "friendly" visit to protect American citizens and interests on the island. As Cuba was a part of the Spanish Empire at that time and the U.S. warship had not been invited, its arrival could have been regarded as being a provocative act. A rebellion by Cuban nationalists attempting to gain independence from Spain was then

Right: The wreck of the USS *Maine* remained in Havana Harbor until 1911, when it was refloated by the U.S. Navy and towed out to sea.

being fought and the rebels were receiving American support, even if the United States appears to have been more concerned with its own interests than those of the people of Cuba. There was talk of the United States annexing the island once the Spanish had left, and of taking control of other Spanish possessions, including Puerto Rico, Guam, and the Philippines. With a much more powerful navy at its disposal, the United States would be almost certain to win in the event of a war with the declining Spanish Empire, and the sinking of the *Maine* provided the spark to ignite the conflict.

REMEMBER THE *MAINE*

The *Maine* was launched in 1889 and, even though it was only ten years old when it sank, it was already becoming obsolete. Naval design was advancing rapidly, spurred on by an arms race between Britain and Germany which had resulted in faster, more heavily armed battleships. Nevertheless, the *Maine* was an imposing sight and its loss was regarded as a major blow to the

UNLUCKY "13"

Left: A cartoon showing King Alphonso XIII of Spain about to experience American "retribution" for playing with boats in Cuba.

U.S. Navy. Whatever caused the initial explosion, it led to a second and much larger blast as the powder magazines for the ship's forward guns ignited; it was this second explosion that destroyed much of the front section of the ship. Once it had sunk, some of its superstructure remained above water in Havana Harbor, where the twisted metal of the front part of the ship was clearly visible.

Both the Americans and the Spanish began separate inquiries in the aftermath of the sinking, and the resulting reports reached opposing conclusions. The Americans pointed to evidence that some metal sheets of the hull were bent inward, and interpreted this as showing that the initial explosion had occurred on the exterior of the ship, which, they concluded, could only have been caused by a mine. The Spanish inquiry had been prevented from inspecting the wreck, so instead relied on eyewitness accounts. Nobody who had witnessed the explosion had seen a column of water blown into the air, as might be expected if a mine had hit the ship, leading the Spanish to find that the first explosion had most likely occurred within the ship, possibly as the result of a fire in one of the coal bunkers.

The conclusion of the Spanish inquiry was completely ignored in the United States. Newspapers were already reporting the sinking as if it had definitely been caused by a Spanish mine, and the U.S. inquiry only served to increase the hysteria. In what would later become known as "yellow journalism," sensationalist reports were published which were either exaggerations of the true situation or deliberately misleading in an effort to sway public opinion. It's difficult to know the extent to which such reporting influenced government policy. War hawks such as Theodore Roosevelt, who was an undersecretary in the naval department at the time, had been advocating military action against the Spanish in Cuba for some time. President William McKinley had favored a negotiated settlement followed by a peaceful transition to independence, even though it had become increasingly apparent that Spain had no intention of allowing Cuba to break away from its empire.

Above: The newspaper magnate William Randolph Hearst, who employed "yellow journalism" to gain public support for war against Spain.

One New York newspaper printed the memorable headline "Remember the *Maine*," which became a rallying cry for supporters of war against Spain. As war fever began to grip the American public, attitudes in the U.S. Congress also began to harden and, on April 25, 1898, the United States officially declared war. It was to be an unequal contest. The U.S. Navy easily outgunned the Spanish in a number of naval encounters, and ground invasions were mounted in Cuba and the Philippines. After three months, Spain sued for peace and was forced to cede the Philippines, Puerto Rico, and Guam to America. Cuba became an American protectorate before achieving full independence a few years later.

SABOTAGE?

Neither the American nor Spanish inquiries appear to have considered the possibility of sabotage. This scenario suggests that a bomb planted by U.S. agents near the ship's magazines caused the powder to ignite, leading to the huge second explosion that sank the vessel. Nothing has ever come to light to support this theory and, in truth, it is most likely based solely on the idea that the United States wanted to incite a war with Spain, rather than being extrapolated from any actual evidence. Would the United States government really have sacrificed one of its battleships and its crew when there must surely have been easier ways to provoke the Spanish?

One conspiracy theory has even suggested that the newspaper magnate William Randolph Hearst was behind the sinking. The theory is based on an apocryphal story of a telegram Hearst is said to have sent to an illustrator for one of his newspapers, who was based in Havana. After the illustrator had cabled Hearst asking to come home because no war appeared likely, he is said to have replied, "You furnish the pictures. I'll furnish the war." Hearst denied sending such a cable but, even if he had, it hardly represents evidence of his complicity in sabotage; more likely it refers to his intention to use yellow journalism in an effort to sway Congress and public opinion.

In 1911, the wreck of the *Maine* was refloated by the U.S. Navy because it was a hazard to shipping in Havana Harbor. It was then towed out to sea and sunk in deep water. The wreck has been investigated on a number of occasions since, without a definite answer being established to the question of what caused the explosions. This means that while an American conspiracy to start the Spanish–American War is highly unlikely, it also can't be entirely ruled out.

—ALTERNATIVE—
THEORIES

An investigation carried out in 2002 for a TV documentary made by the Discovery Channel used photographic evidence obtained by divers from the deep-water wreck of the *Maine* to confirm some of the findings of the initial American inquiry, in particular, that portions of the ship's hull were bent inward. Rather than conclude that this was caused by an exploding mine, the new investigation thought that the metal sheets of the hull could have been bent inward by the force of inrushing water entering the ship after the huge second explosion, a scenario which the researchers demonstrated as a possibility in a series of laboratory experiments.

When this information was combined with a study of archival material, including the original plans of the ship, the investigation concluded that the most likely cause of the initial explosion was a fire in one of the ship's forward coal bunkers. Such a fire—a known hazard in coal-powered ships—could have started spontaneously. It was

Above: The USS *Maine*. By the time of the sinking in 1898, advances in naval technology meant that the ship had become obsolete.

determined that the copper kegs used to store powder in the ship's forward magazines were positioned right up against the bulkheads, making an explosion an accident waiting to happen. In the original inquiry, it was suggested, the U.S. Navy had preferred not to entertain the idea that the explosion had been caused through poor design and negligence, instead pointing to an external source for which the navy could not be blamed.

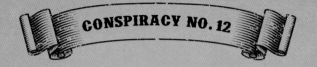

WHO WAS TO BLAME FOR THE SINKING OF THE *LUSITANIA*?

Date: May 7, 1915
Location: Off the south coast of Ireland

RMS *Lusitania* was sunk by a German U-boat in 1915. Theorists have speculated ever since that Britain may have deliberately put the ship at risk of attack for its own ends.

At the start of the First World War in August 1914, Britain had used its superior naval power to impose a blockade on Germany to prevent any merchant ships bringing war materials into German ports. The blockade obstructed ships carrying food, a move considered by Germany to be illegal under international law. The following February, after it had become clear that the war would be a protracted one, Germany retaliated by declaring unrestricted submarine warfare against enemy shipping in British waters, including merchant ships as well as naval vessels. A passenger ship like the *Lusitania* should have remained protected and been able to travel freely under international law unless it was also carrying war materials as cargo, in which case it could legally be stopped and sunk after the passengers and crew had been given the chance to abandon the ship in lifeboats.

THE LAST VOYAGE

Before the *Lusitania* left New York on May 1, 1915, to make the Atlantic crossing to Liverpool, the German embassy in Washington placed notices in American newspapers warning of the potential dangers of sailing through British waters where German submarines were

Above: An illustration of the moment the *Lusitania* was struck by a torpedo fired by the German U-boat U-20.

operating. In spite of these warnings, the ship departed with almost 2,000 passengers and crew on board. At the time, ships like the *Lusitania* were not thought to be vulnerable to submarine attack because of their size and speed and, as it entered British waters off the coast of Ireland, the ocean liner was not provided with a naval escort.

In the days leading up to the sinking of the *Lusitania*, a German U-boat had attacked a number of British merchant ships to the south of Ireland, sinking several of them. Warnings were issued by the British admiralty to all shipping in plenty of time for the *Lusitania* to have been either rerouted to the north of Ireland or to sail closer to the Irish coast, where a submarine was unlikely to be positioned because it could have been spotted from the shore. For whatever reason, the *Lusitania* kept to its course about 10 miles off the coast, where it was intercepted by a U-boat. The captain of the U-boat recorded in his log firing one torpedo at the ship, which hit it under the bridge and exploded. A second and much larger explosion followed, causing the ship to list badly and then, after a further 18 minutes, to sink. It was equipped with more than enough lifeboats to hold everybody on board, but the angle of the list and the speed with which the ship sank meant that many of the lifeboats were never launched. In the end, 1,198 lives were lost.

Most of the people who died were either British or Canadian, but 128 were American citizens. The event led to a major diplomatic incident between the United States and Germany, which would lead to the Germans suspending their campaign of unrestricted submarine warfare. It did not provoke the United States into declaring war on Germany, as the British may have hoped it would, but it did contribute to a rising tide of anti-German feeling in America, and this would play a part in the United States' decision to enter the war two years later.

Above: The *Lusitania* docked in New York. The ship departed New York on May 1, 1915, on what would be its last voyage.

BRITISH SECRETS

After the sinking, the Germans claimed that the *Lusitania* had been carrying contraband war materials, making it a legitimate target. The cargo list included rifle ammunition, which did not contravene the regulations on what a passenger ship could carry, but the nature of the second explosion suggested the presence of undeclared items such as explosives and munitions. Whatever the case, the lack of precautions taken by the British to protect the *Lusitania* from attack certainly gives the impression that either a terrible mistake had been made or the British really were prepared to put the ship at risk to encourage the United States to enter the war.

The radio communications between the *Lusitania* and the British authorities in the two days before it sank were not made available to the inquiry held to determine what had happened. This could have been because the British did not want to reveal the strategy they were using to avoid submarines, but it could also have been part of a cover-up, implemented either to hide incompetence or because the ship had intentionally been put

— ALTERNATIVE —
THEORIES

One possible reason why the *Lusitania* may not have been warned of submarine activity off the Irish coast could have been to prevent Germany from discovering that the British had broken German naval codes and were intercepting and deciphering radio transmissions to U-boats. The cryptography section of the Royal Navy, based in Room 40 of the Old Admiralty Building in London, was top secret, and the British may have been concerned that, should the Lusitania suddenly start taking evasive action to avoid a submarine, the Germans would realize that the locations of their U-boats were known because their radio transmissions

Above: The Old Admiralty Building in Whitehall, now known as the Ripley Building. The top-secret Room 40 was originally on the first floor.

were not secure. This may also explain the secrecy surrounding the radio transmissions sent to the *Lusitania*, though not why these transmissions still remain secret today.

at risk. The fact that, more than a hundred years later, these communications have still not been released, long after the need for operational secrecy, certainly suggests that the British authorities were hiding something, but, while such secrecy continues, it remains impossible to know for certain if the ship and so many lives were deliberately sacrificed.

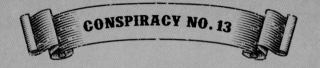

WAS THE UNITED STATES EXPECTING THE ATTACK ON PEARL HARBOR?

Date: December 7, 1941
Location: Oahu, Hawaii

According to one conspiracy theory, the United States had advance knowledge of the Japanese attack on Pearl Harbor, but allowed it to go ahead, sacrificing thousands of lives for strategic gain.

The attack on the U.S. naval base was allowed to happen, the theory alleges, to provide President Franklin D. Roosevelt with the act of unprovoked Japanese aggression he required in order for him to take the United States into the Second World War. Almost all historians of the period reject this theory, arguing that it is not backed up by any substantive evidence. They also question whether a U.S. president would really be prepared to put thousands of American lives and the U.S. Navy's entire Pacific fleet at risk to achieve an aim that could surely have been better accomplished by other means. A variation of the theory alleges that it was actually the British who knew about the attack from intercepted communications they had decrypted, but they did not pass on the information because they wanted the United States to be dragged into the war. But

Right: Three U.S. battleships under attack at Pearl Harbor. The USS *Arizona*, on the right, was sunk with the loss of 1,177 lives.

are either of these theories actually based on anything concrete, or were both fabricated by people who prefer to believe that conspiracies are behind every major world event?

ROOSEVELT'S WAR

The Japanese attack on the morning of December 7, 1941, caught the Americans at Pearl Harbor completely by surprise. Tensions between the two countries had been rising for some time and general warnings had been issued to all U.S. military bases in the Pacific about the possibility of an attack, but no specific mention had been made of Pearl Harbor. Despite the presence of a large proportion of the U.S. Navy's Pacific fleet, there appears to have been an assumption that the Japanese would not dare to launch a strike against the base. In total, 2,403 people were killed in the attack and nineteen ships were sunk, five of them battleships.

The following day President Roosevelt addressed a joint session of Congress, famously describing the attack as "a date which will live in infamy" and asking for a declaration of war against Japan. The declaration was voted through both houses of Congress within the hour. The Tripartite Pact that existed between Japan, Germany, and Italy meant that a declaration of war against one would lead to war with the other two, so the United States had, in effect, entered the Second World War on the side of the Allies. Up until that point, public opinion had been firmly against war and, as part of his campaign during the presidential election in the previous year, Roosevelt had made a commitment not to involve the United States in any foreign wars. In the aftermath of the attack on Pearl Harbor, public opinion swung to the opposite extreme. The United States had been attacked by Japan and, in declaring war, Roosevelt was simply defending the homeland. If Roosevelt really had been looking for a reason to go to war, then he had certainly found one.

Below: President Roosevelt signing the declaration of war against Japan on December 8, 1941, the day after the attack on Pearl Harbor.

Allegations that Roosevelt had allowed the attack on Pearl

Harbor to happen so he could declare war began to surface before the Second World War was over. He had, according to the theory, used Pearl Harbor as bait to encourage a Japanese attack in the knowledge that war with Japan would also mean war with Germany. A diary entry made by Henry L. Stimson, the Secretary of War, ten days before Pearl Harbor, gives an indication that there was at least some basis to the theory. Stimson wrote about a conversation with the president in which Roosevelt had said he thought the Japanese were likely to attack in the near future. The diary entry continued, "The question was how we should maneuver them into the position of firing the first shot without too much danger to ourselves." Stimson made no mention in his diary entry of Pearl Harbor, and would later write in his memoirs of the shock he had felt after learning how unprepared the naval base had been. This suggests that he, and most likely Roosevelt as well, did not have prior knowledge of a specific attack on Pearl Harbor and, in particular, of the size and scale of the attack that occurred.

Above: Churchill meeting with Roosevelt in August 1941. Did Churchill withhold intelligence about the attack on Pearl Harbor from the Americans?

In any case, if the president had known about it, there was no reason why he would want to prevent warnings from being issued. Any sort of Japanese military action against U.S. territory would have been sufficient to justify an American response. So, had the naval base at Pearl Harbor been warned and properly prepared so that it could have fought off the attack with few casualties, the strike would still have constituted grounds for the United States to go to war.

A FAILURE OF INTELLIGENCE

By December 1941 the British had made progress in breaking Japanese diplomatic codes, leading to speculation that radio messages about the attack on Pearl Harbor had been intercepted and deciphered but the British prime minister Winston Churchill decided not to pass the intelligence on to the Americans. No evidence has been found to back up these accusations, though the many the secret files relating to code-breaking have never been made public. In any case, in order to maintain secrecy the Japanese military planners of the attack appear not to have informed their foreign office about it, and strict radio silence was observed by the force carrying out the attack to minimize the possibility of any

Above: A Japanese cipher machine, known as "Purple" to the American code-breakers who cracked the code used to send Japanese diplomatic messages.

radio messages being intercepted. Churchill, then, rather than withholding intelligence from the United States, probably had little of value to pass on.

American code-breakers had also deciphered Japanese diplomatic codes, but, like the British, had not uncovered any specific threats to Pearl Harbor. Nevertheless, enough intelligence had been gathered to warn of some sort of attack and, had this been put together with information gathered from other sources, such as agents on the ground noticing increased Japanese interest in Pearl Harbor, it should have become apparent that an attack was being planned. Unfortunately, there appears to have been little coordination between the different intelligence agencies involved, so the information was not put together and no specific warnings were given out. Even so, Pearl Harbor was a vital military base and its commanders should not have allowed it to be quite so unprepared. In the aftermath of the attack, both the navy and army commanders of the base were dismissed from their posts for dereliction of duty.

The United States' failure to prevent the attack on Pearl Harbor, then, appears to have had more to do with overconfidence and negligence than conspiracy. The Americans simply did not believe the Japanese were capable of attacking a target so far from Japan or that they would dare to undertake such a high-risk mission. On both counts, the United States was proved to be wrong.

— ALTERNATIVE —
THEORIES

Neither of the three American aircraft carriers of the U.S. Pacific fleet—*Enterprise*, *Lexington*, and *Saratoga*—were at Pearl Harbor on December 7, 1941, leading to conspiracy theorists suggesting that these ships were considered too important to risk and had been taken out to sea shortly before the attack. In fact, the *Enterprise* and *Lexington* were both on operations to transport aircraft to the islands of Wake and Midway, two American possessions in the Pacific Ocean closer to Japan than Hawaii and thought to be more at risk. The *Saratoga* had been away from the fleet for almost a year, undergoing an extensive refit, and at the time of the attack was at the naval base in San Diego to pick up its aircraft.

None of the carriers, then, had been taken out of Pearl Harbor shortly before the attack. Even if this had been the case, it begs the question of why—had the Americans known of the attack—would they have left six

Above: "Battleship Row": U.S. battleships moored line astern at Pearl Harbor, making them an easy target for Japanese planes to attack.

battleships in the firing line? At that time, battleships were considered to be the most important ships in the navy. If there had really been prior knowledge of the Japanese attack, surely proper preparations would have been undertaken to protect them.

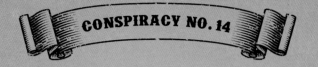

DID THE FSB CARRY OUT THE RUSSIAN APARTMENT BOMBINGS?

Date: September 1999
Location: Buynaksk, Moscow, and Volgodonsk, Russia

In September 1999, a series of explosions rocked three Russian cities. The government blamed Islamic terrorists, but some believe the Russian security service was really behind the attacks.

The first bomb went off on September 4 in the city of Buynaksk in Dagestan, in the Caucasus region of the Russian Federation. This was followed by two bombs on September 9 and 13 in Moscow, and a fourth in Volgodonsk, a city in the Black Sea region, three days later. At least three other bombs were discovered and defused in Moscow and then, on September 22, yet another was found and disarmed in Ryazan, a city to the south of the capital. The police in the city had been alerted to suspicious behavior in an apartment block and found a similar device to those used in the previous attacks.

PUTIN'S WAR

All of the bombs had been principally composed of the high explosive known as RDX. Altogether, around three hundred people were killed in the attacks and many more injured. The Russian government blamed Chechen rebels for the explosions, and the day after the bomb had been found in Ryazan, Russian air attacks began on Grozny, the capital of Chechnya. The attacks were ordered by Vladimir Putin, who had been appointed as prime minster in President Boris Yeltsin's government in August 1999, having previously served as the director of the FSB (the Russian Federal Security Service). A week later, the Russian army began a ground offensive against Chechnya in what became the Second Chechen War. The first war, fought from December 1994 to August 1996, had been an attempt to force Chechnya back into the Russian Federation after it had declared independence in 1991 during the dissolution of the Soviet Union. The war had proved disastrous for the Russians, who had been forced to accept a peace settlement in which Chechnya remained independent.

Above: The huge bomb blast at an apartment block in Volgodonsk on September 16, 1999, caused extensive damage and resulted in seventeen deaths.

On September 24, two days after the bomb was found in Ryazan, police in the city arrested three people in connection with the bombing, all of whom turned out to be FSB operatives. The Russian government ordered that all three be released without charge; the official explanation for their actions was that they had been on an FSB training exercise. The purpose of such training, in which a bomb composed of extremely dangerous high explosives had been placed in an apartment block full of people, was not made clear.

Russian military success in Chechnya boosted Putin, who had not previously been a widely known political figure. After Yeltsin unexpectedly resigned the presidency in December, Putin became acting president and went on to win the subsequent presidential election in March 2000. He then issued a decree granting Yeltsin immunity against charges of corruption and stopped an ongoing investigation into his own conduct.

FSB INVOLVEMENT

In such circumstances, it is hardly surprising to find Putin's political opponents alleging that not only was the Ryazan bomb the work of the FSB, but that all of the others had also been planted as part of a conspiracy to give the Russian government the justification and public support it needed to go to war in Chechnya for the second time. The official inquiry rejected all such allegations and named Ibn al-Khattab as the ringleader of the bombings, claiming that he was a member of the Islamic extremist group al-Qaeda. The Saudi-born Khattab was a military leader with a Chechen separatist group who, before being assassinated by the FSB in 2002, denied any involvement in the bombings or affiliation with al-Qaeda.

An independent inquiry set up by Sergei Kovalev, a deputy in the Russian parliament, and led by the prominent lawyer Mikhail Trepashkin, uncovered potential links between the FSB and the other bombings as well as the failed attempt in Ryazan. FSB officers, it was alleged, had provided the RDX used in the explosions and, in one case, had rented a basement apartment in one of the buildings in Moscow where a bomb had exploded. A few days before the findings of the investigation were presented to a Russian court, Trepashkin was arrested by the FSB for revealing state secrets, convicted by a closed military court and sentenced to four years in prison.

The Russian authorities subsequently named a number of Chechen suspects in the bombings, almost all of whom were either killed in the Second Chechen War or assassinated by the FSB. The few who were captured were tried in secret and

— ALTERNATIVE —
THEORIES

A more elaborate conspiracy theory concerning the apartment bombings alleges that they were actually a key part of an FSB-led plot to oust Yeltsin from the presidency and replace him with Putin in what was, in effect, a coup d'état. The public outrage following the bombings allowed Putin to take Russia to war in Chechnya and he used the popularity he gained from its success to maneuver himself into a position to succeed Yeltsin. It has further been alleged that Putin then used evidence of corruption gathered by the FSB against Yeltsin and members of his family to force him to resign the presidency, opening the way for Putin to stand in the subsequent elections.

Above: President Boris Yeltsin resigned in December 1999, allowing Vladimir Putin to stand in the presidential elections held in March 2000.

sentenced to long jail terms. A proper inquiry would be required to determine exactly what happened and what role the FSB played, but it is hard to envisage such an investigation taking place while Vladimir Putin remains in power. As the Russian constitution has been changed to allow him to continue as president until at least 2024, this situation is not likely to change in the foreseeable future.

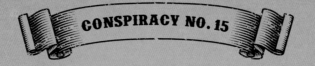

WAS THE UNITED STATES GOVERNMENT INVOLVED IN 9/11?

Date: September 11, 2001
Location: USA

In the wake of 9/11, 2,996 people were killed. The official version of events is that al-Qaeda coordinated the attacks, but some accuse the U.S. government and security services of involvement.

The "9/11 truthers," as the people who dispute the official version are sometimes known, believe the U.S. government and security services either had prior knowledge of the attacks and did nothing to prevent them or actually carried out the attacks themselves. They contend that the purpose of the attacks was to enable the U.S. government to go to war in the Middle East in order to gain control of the region's oil resources and also to create conditions in the United States which would allow the government to restrict civil liberties. Numerous strands of evidence have been proposed to support such accusations, the most commonly expressed being that the Twin Towers of the World Trade Center in New York and 7 World Trade Center, the third building to collapse, were not brought down as a result of the impact of two airliners; rather

Right: An aerial view shows the huge quantity of dust thrown up by the collapse of the Twin Towers in New York.

all three were demolished by controlled explosions. It has also been alleged that the Pentagon was hit by an American missile, not an airliner, and that the fourth airliner to be hijacked, which crashed in Pennsylvania, did not do so because passengers attempted to fight off the hijackers, but was actually shot down by a U.S. Air Force plane.

TRUTH OR FANTASY?

Truthers have largely based their allegations on perceived inconsistencies in the official version of the attacks, together with alternative interpretations of the available evidence. But is there any substance to these allegations, or are they solely based on what the truthers want to believe? After all, if any one of the allegations can be backed up with indisputable evidence, then senior political, military, and intelligence leaders, going all the way up to President George W. Bush, would be implicated in a huge conspiracy that resulted in the deaths of almost three thousand people and led to wars in which hundreds of thousands more were killed.

An investigation into the collapse of the Twin Towers by the National Institute of Standards and Technology (NIST) concluded that all of the towers were brought down because uncontrolled fires had undermined key structural elements of the buildings. The initial impact of the two airliners into the towers and the resulting explosions had stripped the fireproofing from the girders which formed the frames of the buildings, leaving steel exposed to very high temperatures generated by the fires. Steel trusses supporting the ceilings buckled,

Above: The explosion caused by the impact of the hijacked airliner with the World Trade Center's South Tower. The North Tower had already been hit.

causing the ceilings to sag and pull the main supporting columns on the exteriors of the building inward, until these were no longer capable of supporting the weight of the floors above. Once the collapse had started, it set off what was, in effect, a chain reaction to bring both the towers down.

A separate inquiry examined the collapse of 7 World Trade Center, which was not hit by an airliner, and found that the building had been extensively damaged by debris falling from the Twin Towers. This caused uncontrolled fires which compromised one of the main supporting columns of the building. The unusual design of the building, a consequence of its location above an electricity generating plant, meant that the loss of one main column weakened the building to such an extent that it collapsed.

The collapse of 7 World Trade Center, which came down about seven hours after the Twin Towers, has been the central tenet of the truthers' claim that all three buildings were brought down by controlled explosions, not least because it remains the only

Right: Debris from American Airlines Flight 77 lying in front of the Pentagon building minutes after the hijacked airliner had crashed into it.

steel-framed tower to have collapsed solely as a consequence of fire. The contention is that a fire simply could not have undermined the structural integrity of any of the three buildings to such an extent that it would cause them to collapse, so there must be an alternative explanation, such as the presence of explosives in the buildings which were then detonated after the airlines crashed. This has been countered by the observation that a controlled demolition would have required an extensive planning phase and large quantities of explosives to be placed in the buildings without arousing the suspicion of the thousands of people who worked in them. The usual way of carrying out tower demolitions is to place explosives at the base of a building, while the Twin Towers very obviously began to collapse from the points where the airliners crashed. As the collapses progressed, windows could be seen blowing out in succession down the buildings. This is taken by truthers as a sign of explosive devices being detonated in sequence, and explained by others as being due to pressure waves formed by the huge weight of falling debris forcing air downward.

Above: Ground Zero—the remains of the Twin Towers, which conspiracy theorists allege were brought down by a controlled demolition.

A convincing argument against the controlled demolition theory is that there was no need for any plan to be so complicated. A single hijacked plane crashing into one building would surely have provided any conspirators with more than enough reason to take retaliatory action against the supposed perpetrators, so why go to the length of organizing a much more complicated plot? It is also hard to understand why it would have been necessary for conspirators to demolish 7 World Trade Center as well as the Twin Towers, or what possible reason there could have been for waiting seven hours before bringing it down.

The controlled demolition theory, then, does not bear a great deal of scrutiny and, in truth, neither do the other main allegations. Eyewitnesses saw an airliner not a missile crash into the Pentagon, and debris from the plane, together with the DNA of some of the passengers, was found at the scene. And, if the airliner did not crash, where is it now and what happened to the passengers? Phone calls made by passengers on board the fourth hijacked airplane, who knew the other three hijacked planes had crashed, contain details of their intention to try to take back control of the plane. What appears to have happened is that once a fight between hijackers and passengers began, the hijacker piloting the airliner intentionally flew it into the ground. No evidence exists of U.S. Air Force planes being in the vicinity at the time or of the airliner having been shot down.

As well as the evidence on the ground, senior leaders of al-Qaeda, including Osama bin Laden, acknowledged their responsibility for

Right: The Taliban's refusal to hand over al-Qaeda members implicated in the 9/11 attacks resulted in the American-led invasion of Afghanistan.

the attacks. This implies that if there was a conspiracy involving the U.S. government, it must have been working together with al-Qaeda. This would appear to be highly unlikely, not least because it would have given al-Qaeda the opportunity to do huge political damage to the United States by revealing the connection. Overall, we are left with a great deal of evidence to show that the incident unfolded as the official version states and nothing credible to undermine this version of events. Like many conspiracy theories, allegations that the U.S. government planned and executed the attacks on 9/11 appear to be based on unfounded speculation and a selective use of the known facts.

INTELLIGENCE FAILINGS

In the months leading up to 9/11, intelligence gathered by a number of different American agencies, including the CIA and NSA (National Security Agency), and by the security services of a number of other countries, pointed toward the possibility of an al-Qaeda plan to attack the United States, which involved the hijacking of planes. The CIA, for instance, knew the identities of two of the hijackers who piloted the airliners and of their intentions to travel to the United States, but failed to pass the information on to the the FBI so they could be prevented from entering the country. Meanwhile, the FBI were aware of an al-Qaeda plan to send people to civil aviation colleges in the United States, yet nothing was done to check the identities of foreign nationals attending any such colleges. It is always easy to be wise in hindsight, but if these two strands of intelligence had been brought together and followed up, then the 9/11 attacks might never have happened.

Some believe that the lack of action taken in response to the intelligence gathered was intentional, and the attacks were allowed to go ahead to provide the United States government with the justification it needed to invade Afghanistan. According to some, this was part of an all-encompassing plot to allow the United States to begin a war that could then be expanded across the Middle East, with the purpose of gaining control of the world's oil supplies. Even grander theories suggest that the attacks were planned by the so-called global elite as part of a conspiracy to establish a New World Order with total control of the world's financial systems.

No evidence has ever come to light to back up any of these conspiracy theories and, in truth, it appears more likely that the attacks were not prevented because of a series of intelligence failings. The inquiries into 9/11 have been highly critical of the agencies for not sharing information among themselves, thus preventing an overall picture of the imminent danger from emerging. Needless to say, truthers and conspiracy theorists do not accept such a scenario, but, whatever they may think, the evidence as it stands suggests that the only conspiracy involved in 9/11 was the one hatched by Osama bin Laden and al-Qaeda.

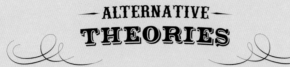

— ALTERNATIVE —
THEORIES

A few hours after the attacks on the Twin Towers, a group of five men were reported to the police because of their strange behavior. They were seen by a number of people standing on top of a white van parked on the New Jersey side of the Hudson River, filming the aftermath of the attacks. They were described as dancing around, and laughing and joking together as if they had something to celebrate. All five men, who turned out to be Israeli citizens, were arrested by police. They were held in custody for more than two months and interrogated on a number of occasions before being deported to Israel.

The police gathered little from questioning the "dancing Israelis," as they have become known, beyond the belief that at least two of them were agents for Mossad, the Israeli secret service. No explanation for their behavior was forthcoming, but, as no links could be established between them and the attacks, there were also no grounds for them to be charged with any crime.

Above: The logo of Mossad, the Israeli secret service. Two of its agents are thought to have been among the five "dancing Israelis" arrested on 9/11.

Conspiracy theorists have cited this incident as indicating that Mossad was either responsible for the attacks or had prior knowledge of them. But if this was the case, then publicly celebrating would have been a very stupid thing for the men to do. It was undoubtedly a bizarre incident, and remains unexplained, but it requires a huge leap to take it as evidence of Israeli complicity in 9/11.

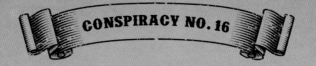

DID IRAQ REALLY POSSESS WEAPONS OF MASS DESTRUCTION?

Date: 2003
Location: USA and UK

Reports that Saddam Hussein possessed weapons of mass destruction were used to justify the Iraq War, but with none ever found, some critics assert that the intelligence was fabricated.

Saddam Hussein had undoubtedly possessed weapons of mass destruction in the past, because he had used poison gases during the Iran–Iraq War in the late 1980s and against Kurdish people in the north of Iraq in 1988. Western countries had also supplied Iraq with the materials needed to make chemical weapons, together with the military hardware he would use in 1990 to invade Kuwait. After the Gulf War, the United Nations Security Council passed a series of resolutions requiring Iraq to destroy all of its WMDs and to allow UN weapons inspectors, including Dr. David Kelly (see page 48), into the country to ensure this had been done. Saddam engaged in a game of brinkmanship with the UN, obstructing the work of the weapons inspectors for as long as possible and then, when threatened with UN sanctions, allowing them to continue their work.

REPORTS OF WMDS

In the aftermath of the 9/11 attacks in 2001, hawks in the American government of President George W. Bush, particularly Dick Cheney, the vice president, and Donald Rumsfeld, the secretary of defense, argued that the only way to deal with Saddam was to remove him by force. Over the course of the year, attitudes hardened in favor of an invasion of Iraq. It was claimed this was because of links between Saddam and al-Qaeda, and because Saddam's WMDs posed a direct threat to the United States. In April 2002, in what would later become a notorious meeting, the British prime minister, Tony Blair, gave his support to President Bush. Later that year, both the United States and the United Kingdom produced intelligence reports backing up claims that Iraq still had stockpiles of chemical and biological weapons, and was attempting to develop a nuclear bomb and long-range missiles.

Above: Saddam Hussein, pictured here in 2004, played a game of brinkmanship with the UN by refusing to allow weapons inspectors into Iraq.

In November 2002, a UN resolution was passed giving Saddam a last chance to fully comply with the previous resolutions or face "serious consequences." It did not specify what these consequences would be, but the implication that military action was an option was clear enough. It was also apparent that, in order to be certain that military action was legal, a further resolution authorizing it was required. Russia, France, and China, three of the five permanent members of the UN Security Council along with the United States and the United Kingdom, all announced they would veto such a resolution because the weapons inspectors needed more time to complete their work. Despite this, the United States and the United Kingdom, together with token forces from a few

Above: Protestors pose as George Bush and Tony Blair with blood on their hands at a Stop the War demonstration held in London in July 2016.

other countries, launched an invasion of Iraq in March 2003, using overwhelming force to defeat Saddam in a matter of weeks.

THE CASE FOR WAR

In international law, there are only two ways for military action to be legal in the absence of a UN resolution: military intervention can be used to prevent a humanitarian crisis or it can be used in defense when one country is attacked by another. The first of these clearly could not be applied to the situation in Iraq, so Bush and Blair attempted to make the case that Saddam represented enough of a direct and immediate threat to the United States and Britain to justify military action. Allegations have been made ever since that they conspired together to manipulate the intelligence to strengthen their case, in the knowledge that it had either been enhanced or completely fabricated.

One claim to which the United States attached particular importance was that Iraq possessed mobile biological weapons laboratories where such deadly toxins as anthrax were being produced. This intelligence had come from an informant codenamed "Curveball," an Iraqi defector living in Germany who claimed to have worked in Iraq's biological weapons programme. Despite warnings from German intelligence that Curveball was not reliable, Colin Powell, then U.S. secretary of state, gave prominence to this information in a speech he made to the UN in February 2003 setting out the case for military action. After the invasions, no mobile laboratories of any sort were found, and it would later emerge that Curveball had in fact been a taxi driver in Baghdad before fleeing to Germany.

— ALTERNATIVE —
THEORIES

Some commentators have alleged that disarming Saddam of WMDs was merely a pretext for gaining control of the country's oil resources. They believe that this was part of a wider strategy by George Bush's administration aimed at maintaining American control of a large proportion of the world's oil supply. The emergence of China as a potential economic rival to the United States in the 1990s is said to have given impetus to these plans, because the Chinese economy was, and remains, reliant on oil imports. President Bush and key members of his administration also had close ties with American oil companies, though

Above: Khor Al Amaya Oil Terminal in Iraq. Many people remain convinced the Iraq War was fought to gain control of the country's oil reserves.

no evidence exists to indicate that such associations really did play any part in the decision to go to war in Iraq.

Much of the rest of the intelligence contained in the American and British reports proved to be no more reliable than that obtained from Curveball. As key information relating to the intelligence remains classified, it is still unclear whether this was a failure by the intelligence services or whether senior political leaders were responsible for starting a war in which hundreds of thousands of people were killed based on information they knew to be false.

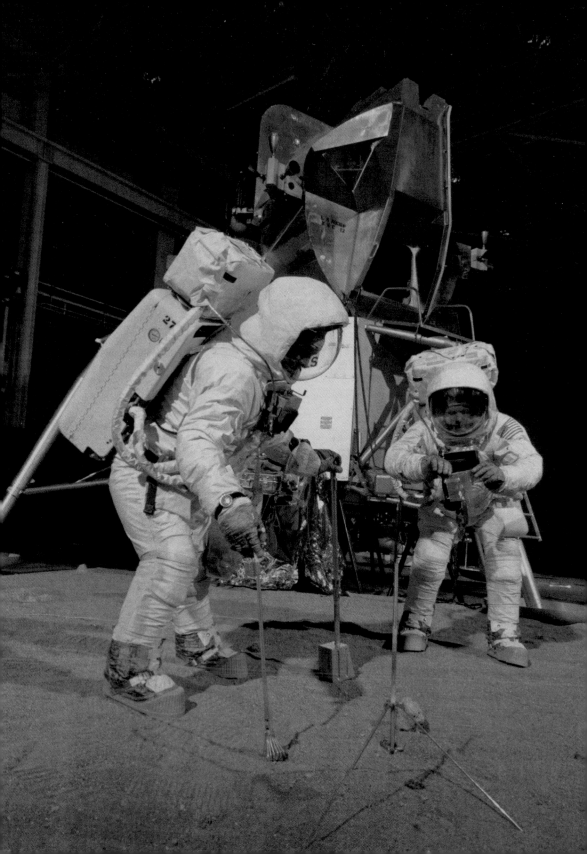

COVER-UPS

M any conspiracies involve secret plots hatched for gain. But there is another type, one which has the principal purpose of preventing evidence of illegal activity or information which may prove damaging from being revealed. This is the cover-up, and in this section we take a look at a number of examples which, for one reason or another, have yet to be fully resolved.

Some of the conspiracies dealt with here undoubtedly did occur, but the full extent of what happened remains unknown. In the Iran–Contra affair, for instance, a conspiracy by members of President Ronald Reagan's administration was discovered and, in the ensuing attempts at

a cover-up, enough government documents were shredded to make it impossible to determine how much Reagan himself knew about what had been going on.

As well as known cover-ups, we examine a number that are alleged to have taken place. While maintaining a healthy degree of skepticism over some of the more outlandish claims, we attempt to unravel the truth behind accusations that NASA faked the moon landings and has been lying about it ever since, and whether aliens really did land at Roswell. Back on firmer ground, we discuss whether the Catholic Church has attempted to conceal its involvement in helping Nazi war criminals escape justice, and if evidence of a conspiracy to destroy the streetcar systems of U.S. cities was suppressed to protect the interests of those involved.

Left: Buzz Aldrin (left) and Neil Armstrong training for the Apollo 11 mission.

DID JESUS AND MARY MAGDALENE MARRY AND HAVE CHILDREN?

Date: first century CE
Location: Galilee and Judea

A prominent theory claims that, rather than being single and celibate, Jesus was married to Mary Magdalene and the pair even had children together. Could their descendants live on today?

In this version of the story, Mary Magdalene is presented as being a much more important figure to Jesus and the development of his teachings than can be gathered from the New Testament, but she was marginalized during the development of Christianity because the early Church was dominated by men. Some conspiracy theorists have gone further, claiming that a marriage between Jesus and Mary Magdalene, and the existence of children, was known to a select few right from the beginnings of Christianity, and a conspiracy of silence has been maintained ever since.

THE HISTORICAL JESUS

Almost all of what we know about the life of Jesus comes from the details provided by the four gospels of the New Testament,

Right: Jesus appears to Mary Magdalene after the Resurrection in a painting by the Russian artist Alexander Andreyevich Ivanov.

Matthew, Mark, Luke, and John, together with other parts of the Bible, such as the epistles of Paul. It is generally accepted that these were written in the late first century CE, beginning about three decades after Jesus had been crucified. A number of other gospels that were not included in the New Testament and were written at somewhat later dates also provide some details of his life, and the works of the early historians Josephus and Tacitus, both writing at the end of the first century CE, mention him on a few occasions. Taken together, these writings are enough to convince most historians of the early Church that a wandering preacher named Jesus existed and lived in the region of Judea, even if no physical evidence has survived to confirm his existence.

The books of the New Testament have almost nothing to say about the life of Jesus between his birth in Bethlehem and his emergence as a wandering preacher at the age of about thirty, after his baptism by John the Baptist. Jesus had a number of brothers and sisters and, at an early age, he is said to have debated Jewish law in the temple, to the amazement of his family. Before becoming

Left: Pages from the Gospel of Thomas (left) and the Secret Book of John (right) found in 1945 near Nag Hammadi in Egypt.

a preacher, he worked as a carpenter in Nazareth, but there is no mention of him getting married or having children.

Even less is known about the life of Mary Magdalene. All that the New Testament tells us is that she became a follower of Jesus after he cleansed her of the "seven demons," and that she witnessed the Crucifixion and Resurrection. The meaning of the seven demons is by no means clear, but from about the sixth century CE it has been used by some in the Church to infer that Mary Magdalene had been a prostitute before meeting Jesus, and had repented for her sins. This could be regarded either as being a reasonable interpretation of the scripture or as an attempt to stain the reputation of Mary Magdalene as part of wider efforts to belittle the importance of the female followers of Jesus. Arguments of this sort have been used to support the dominance of men in the churches of all denominations from the earliest period, which has only begun to be challenged in

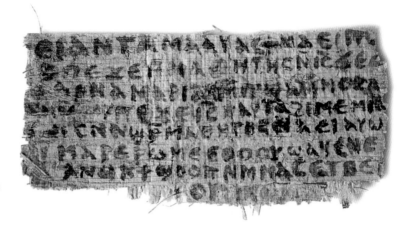

Right: The papyrus fragment described by Professor Karen King as the Gospel of Jesus's Wife, now thought to be a modern forgery.

recent years; though, rather than being an intentional conspiracy, it could simply be a reflection of the patriarchal nature of those societies in which Christianity developed.

A DIFFERENT MARY

In some early Christian writings not included in the New Testament, such as the Gnostic gospels of Thomas and Philip, Mary Magdalene is presented in a rather different light. She is described as being the companion of Jesus and as being the one among all of his followers who best understood his teaching. The use of the word "companion" to describe the relationship between Jesus and Mary Magdalene is certainly intriguing, but it does not necessarily imply that they were married. In fact, there is no mention of Mary Magdalene being the wife of Jesus or of the existence of any children in any of the Gnostic gospels.

The most complete copies we have of the gospels of Philip and Thomas were both found in 1945 buried in a jar near the Egyptian town of Nag Hammadi. The manuscripts in what has become known as the Nag Hammadi library have been dated to the fourth century CE and are almost certainly copies of earlier works. While they do not provide evidence of Jesus being married and having children, they do show that different interpretations existed of the role played by Mary Magdalene, and of women in general, in the life of Jesus and the early Church than those presented in the New Testament.

In 2012, Professor Karen King, the first woman to hold the Hollis Chair of Divinity at Harvard University, announced the discovery of a papyrus fragment which she described as being the Gospel of Jesus's Wife. The surviving text included the name Mary and a partial sentence which reads, "Jesus said to them, 'My wife...'" Professor King thought that the fragment dated to the fourth century CE and could have been copied from a lost gospel. Not enough of it survives to be able to say whether the Mary it mentions was Mary Magdalene, or even if Mary was the name of Jesus's wife. Even so, if it could be shown to be genuine, then it would provide the first clear indication that at least some early Christians believed Jesus to have been married.

Almost as soon as the existence of the fragment became known, questions were raised about its provenance, not least because the occurrence of the name Mary with the word "wife" gave the impression of it being a little too good to be true. An investigation by the journalist Ariel Sabar, published in the *Atlantic* magazine in 2016, presented convincing evidence that the fragment was a modern forgery, by tracing it back to a man who was known to have produced forged ancient manuscripts in the past. Professor King has since accepted that, in all likelihood, the fragment is not real, and it now appears to have been little more than an attempt to cash in on the publicity generated by Dan Brown's 2003 novel *The Da Vinci Code*, which took the possibility of Jesus having direct descendants as its central premise. There remains, then, no definitive evidence that Jesus was married to Mary Magdalene, which means that any theories based on this assumption can only be speculative in nature.

— ALTERNATIVE —
THEORIES

In *The Holy Blood and the Holy Grail*, first published in 1982, Michael Baigent, Richard Leigh, and Henry Lincoln took the idea that Jesus and Mary Magdalene had children and ran with it. They added the Holy Grail, the Knights Templar, and a secret organization called the Priory of Sion to the mix, to develop a theory in which the children of Jesus and Mary Magdalene not only existed but emigrated to France, where their descendants founded the Merovingian dynasty of French kings. Apparently, the Grand Masters of the Priory of Sion kept this knowledge secret for almost a thousand years, having first discovered the truth in 1099.

The Holy Blood and the Holy Grail may or may not have provided the inspiration for Dan Brown's novel *The Da Vinci Code*, depending on which legal arguments are accepted. In 2005, Baigent and Leigh sued Brown, alleging he had stolen the plot from their book. They lost the case, but the publicity they received probably helped to soften the blow.

Above: The Templar Cross, symbol of the Knights Templar, who, according to one theory, were tasked with preserving the secret of Jesus Christ's bloodline.

Long before then, the entire theory had been exposed as a hoax perpetrated by Pierre Plantard. In 1989, Plantard admitted to inventing the Priory of Sion, together with his claim to be its last Grand Master and the direct descendant of the Merovingian kings, which, according to the theory at least, made him a descendant of Jesus. His admission could have ended all the speculation, but, then again, why let the truth stand in the way of a good story?

DID GENERAL MOTORS CONSPIRE TO DESTROY THE STREETCAR SYSTEMS?

Date: 1930s to 1960s
Location: Cities across the USA

By the 1960s, most of the United States' streetcars had been replaced by buses and cars, a change that some think was spearheaded by the companies that stood to benefit.

In the 1920s, when only one in ten people in the United States owned a car, General Motors' long-serving president Alfred Sloan recognized the enormous potential market for private motor vehicles. At that time, many people in cities traveled by streetcar. According to the conspiracy theory, Sloan decided to buy streetcar companies in as many cities across the United States as possible, then run them into the ground and close them down. At the same time, General Motors bought a bus manufacturing company and a bus operating company, allowing the corporation to replace the streetcars with its own buses.

NATIONAL CITY LINES

Beginning in the mid-1920s, General Motors began buying into the extensive streetcar system in New York, which operated numerous

Right: Until the 1930s, most American cities had electric streetcar systems, but by 1940 these had all but disappeared.

routes through the streets of Manhattan, and in several smaller cities, including Springfield, Ohio, and Kalamazoo, Michigan. By 1936, the entire streetcar system in Manhattan had been closed down and replaced by buses. It appears that this success led to a decision to greatly expand the strategy of "motorizing" streetcar systems, and a pattern emerged in which, once companies had been bought and the streetcars replaced with buses, the operating companies were given contracts specifying that they had to buy buses either from General Motors or Mack Trucks, tires from Firestone, and fuel and oil from Standard Oil or Philips Petroleum.

As a means of expanding the scheme, General Motors, together with Standard Oil, Firestone, and the others, began to invest in a small bus company in Minnesota run by E. Roy Fitzgerald, turning it into National City Lines (NCL). Over the course of the following ten years, NCL and its subsidiaries bought up and motorized over a hundred companies in at least forty-five cities, replacing the electric streetcars with diesel-powered buses. In most cases the tracks and electrification systems were ripped up completely, ensuring that it would be difficult and extremely expensive for cities to ever reverse the changes and bring back the streetcars.

During the Second World War, most Americans may have had other things on their minds than the loss of the streetcars, but in its aftermath few people could fail to notice that the streets of many cities were becoming increasingly congested and the air ever more polluted. This cannot be blamed entirely on the loss of the streetcars. Congestion and pollution became a problem in numerous cities across the world as rising populations and greater affluence resulted in an ever-increasing amount of traffic on the roads. But there can be little doubt that the decline of the streetcar, and of mass transit systems in general, was a contributory factor in the United States.

ANTITRUST

In 1946, Edwin J. Quinby, who had worked for a streetcar company in New Jersey that had been closed down before the war, wrote and self-published a pamphlet exposing the ownership and practices of NCL. He sent it to numerous politicians, city mayors, and newspapers across the United States and, despite a smear campaign which attempted to dismiss him as a crank, it led to antitrust charges being brought against General Motors and the other companies that had backed NCL. As there were no laws against anybody buying a company and running it into the ground, the charges related to the way in which the streetcar companies were acquired and supplied, which, it was alleged, excluded competition. All the companies charged were found guilty and fined the token amount of $5,000, while a number of individuals, including E. Roy Fitzgerald, were fined $1 each. It amounted to a very minor slap on the wrist to the companies that had profited enormously from such unscrupulous business dealings, and in no way compensated for the loss of the streetcars.

In recent years, a number of cities which lost their streetcars have reintroduced electrified mass transport systems of one sort or another, mostly streetcars or light railway systems. These have often been installed to serve the same routes where the

— ALTERNATIVE —
THEORIES

A different explanation for the disappearance of streetcars is that, by the end of the 1920s, many of the private companies operating them were not financially viable. Streetcars were expensive because of the costs of maintaining the track and the electrification system; and, at that time, services were regularly interrupted by strikes and power cuts. The beginning of the Great Depression after the Wall Street Crash of 1929 exacerbated the problems and, in any case, an increasing number of people were choosing the convenience of owning their own car over using public transport. So it could be argued that whatever General Motors did or didn't do, the days of the streetcar were coming to an end.

Above: A 1940s advertisement for Cadillac, a division of General Motors. The attraction of personal automobiles was one reason that streetcars disappeared.

old streetcars used to run, and have proved to be popular with passengers, but have cost billions of dollars of public money. Today, the streetcar scandal provides us with an example of what happens when corporate interests are allowed to go unchecked: a small and already wealthy minority of owners and shareholders get richer still, while the less well-off majority of taxpayers have to pick up the bill.

WAS THE PHILADELPHIA EXPERIMENT REAL?

Date: October 1943
Location: Philadelphia, Pennsylvania, USA

In the 1950s, perplexing rumors surfaced that in 1943 the U.S. Navy had conducted a secret experiment in which one of its destroyers was turned invisible.

Numerous different stories about what happened in the Philadelphia Navy Yard, some more credible than others, have circulated over the years. As far as it is possible to tell, the origin of the rumors can be traced back to letters written in 1955 by Carl M. Allen, under the name Carlos Miguel Allende, to Morris K. Jessup, who had recently published a book entitled *The Case for the UFO*. The letters are rambling and somewhat incoherent in nature, but, in a nutshell, Allen tells of how in October 1943, he witnessed the disappearance of the naval destroyer USS *Eldridge* from the dock where it was berthed in Philadelphia. He says he watched the event from the SS *Andrew Furuseth*, the merchant ship he claims to have been serving on at that time.

A HOLE IN SPACE-TIME

As if a destroyer disappearing into thin air was not bizarre enough, Allen went on to claim that, after the *Eldridge* had vanished from

Philadelphia, it appeared for a few seconds at the naval base in Norfolk, Virginia, before reappearing in Philadelphia. Many members of the ship's crew were either killed or did not return when it materialized, and those that did return suffered from a variety of mental disturbances. Because of the terrible cost to the crew, the experiment was never repeated and the U.S. Navy and government covered up what had occurred.

According to the letters, Allen not only witnessed what had happened but could also provide an explanation. The experiment had been based on research carried out in the early 1930s by, among others, Albert Einstein and Nikola Tesla, on unified field theory, a branch

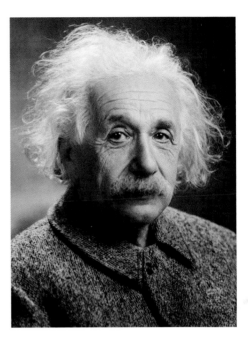

Above: Albert Einstein, whose concept of space-time supposedly provided the theoretical basis for the Philadelphia Experiment.

of theoretical physics which attempts to reconcile Einstein's theory of general relativity with electromagnetism. Relativity describes the gravitational force which acts on the three dimensions of space and the fourth dimension of time. Einstein's great insight was that space and time are not separate, but form a continuum he called space-time. This can be bent by large gravitational fields, such as those formed by stars and planets, implying that time can vary. Electromagnetism, on the other hand, is concerned with the forces between particles inside the atom that give rise to the phenomena of electricity and magnetism.

What Allen appears to have been suggesting is that the experiment involving the *Eldridge* had, perhaps inadvertently, found a way of unifying the fields of relativity and electromagnetism at the scale of a destroyer so that the application of an electric charge bent space-time sufficiently for the ship to disappear. According to Allen, this opened up a hole in space-time which the ship fell through, causing its brief reappearance at the naval base in Norfolk.

Above: Sailors examining a radar scope in 1944. Some think that radar research was being conducted in the Philadelphia Navy Yard.

If Allen's claims are taken seriously, then one or two problems become apparent. Principal among these is the fact that unified field theory continues to elude physicists to this day. If navy scientists had come up with a solution in 1943, it would have represented one of the greatest advances in the whole of science and, if it had been achieved in the way described by Allen, would have provided proof that teleportation and time travel—those two staple ingredients of science fiction—were not only possible but had been demonstrated. It appears unlikely that scientists involved in such earth-shattering research would then shelve it and never revisit it, when public knowledge of the magnitude of their achievement would make them more famous than Einstein.

A STEALTH DESTROYER

A rather more straightforward explanation of what, if anything, happened in the Philadelphia Navy Yard was that the U.S. Navy were investigating ways of using electromagnetic fields to protect ships from the sort of magnetic mines being used by Germany during the Second World War. By 1943, considerable success had been made in reducing the vulnerability of ships to such mines in a process known as degaussing, which involved using electric charges to reduce the disturbance to the Earth's magnetic field caused by a ship, so that it would not set off a mine.

Another possibility is that the navy was conducting experiments into cloaking, in which scientists were attempting to use an electromagnetic field to make ships invisible to enemy radar in a

—ALTERNATIVE—
THEORIES

Not even the slightest shred of evidence exists that anything out of the ordinary occurred in the navy yard at Philadelphia in October 1943, so another explanation for the Philadelphia Experiment is that it never happened. The whole thing was a hoax perpetrated by Carl Allen, with the knowing or unknowing assistance of Morris Jessup, and, once it had begun, the story took on a life of its own. No evidence exists either that Allen served as a U.S. merchant marine or that the SS *Andrew Furuseth* was anywhere near Philadelphia at the time. And, in any case, how likely is it that the navy would carry out top-secret research on cutting-edge technology in the middle of a navy yard where everybody could see it?

Above: The poster for *The Philadelphia Experiment*, a film adaptation of a sci-fi novel loosely based on the story of the *Eldridge*.

similar way to how stealth technology is used today. Such research would obviously be top secret, but it is not difficult to imagine rumors of attempts to make ships invisible to radar spreading and being adapted in the retelling to suggest the purpose was to make the ships invisible to the eye. The navy has always denied that any such research took place in Philadelphia, but then again, they would say that, wouldn't they?

DID THE CATHOLIC CHURCH HELP NAZI WAR CRIMINALS EVADE CAPTURE?

Date: 1948

Location: Europe and South America

After the Second World War, a number of senior Catholic clerics helped Nazi war criminals escape to South America. What remains unclear is exactly who in the Church knew about it.

The number of Nazis to successfully flee Europe after the end of the war is estimated to have been in the region of nine thousand, most of whom traveled through Italy and on to Spain before departing for South America. The right-wing governments in a number of South American countries, including Argentina, Brazil, Uruguay, and Paraguay, were prepared to at least tolerate the presence of Nazis who had been accused of committing war crimes, including some who were implicated in the murder of millions of Jewish people in the Holocaust. Among them was Adolf Eichmann, a high-ranking SS officer who had been responsible for the overall management of the Nazi extermination camps. Others included the senior concentration camp officials Josef Mengele, Franz Stangl, and Horst Wagner, together with a long list of men accused of committing terrible crimes against humanity.

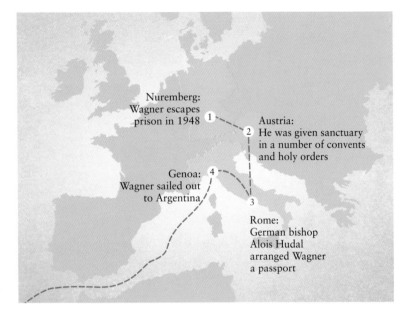

Nuremberg:
Wagner escapes
prison in 1948

Austria:
He was given sanctuary
in a number of convents
and holy orders

Genoa:
Wagner sailed out
to Argentina

Rome:
German bishop
Alois Hudal
arranged Wagner
a passport

Right: The ratline used
by the escaped Nazi war
criminal Horst Wagner,
who traveled to Italy
through Austria and then
on to Argentina.

RATLINES

The escape routes used by escaping Nazis were dubbed "ratlines."
These made use of contacts established during the war between
Catholic clergymen in Spain and their counterparts in a number
of South American countries, and had originally been intended for
the humanitarian purpose of helping Catholic refugees fleeing war-
torn Europe. The primary route involved traveling from Germany
to South Tyrol in Austria, where long-established smuggling routes
were used to cross into Italy.

The Nazi escapees were provided with false identity papers by
sympathizers and stayed in a network of safe houses while they
were traveling. Once they had crossed the Italian border, most
continued on to Rome, where many were provided with assistance
by Bishop Alois Hudal, an Austrian-born cleric who was the head
of a Catholic seminary in Rome and is considered to have been
the informal leader of German and Austrian Catholics in the city.
A number of the Nazis he sheltered later named him as a contact
in Rome. One of these was Franz Stangl, the former commandant

of the Treblinka and Sobibor concentration camps. He described how Hudal helped him acquire the necessary documentation and references from the Vatican to enable him to travel onwards, in his case, first to Syria and then Brazil.

It has been estimated that eight hundred escaping Nazis managed to obtain travel documents from the International Committee of the Red Cross, stating that they were genuine refugees, after clerics such as Bishop Hudal and others in Rome and the Vatican had provided references for them. It has led to allegations that some senior figures in the Red Cross were aware that their system for dealing with refugees was being exploited by Nazi war criminals and turned a blind eye. As there were millions of displaced persons at the end of the war, perhaps it is understandable that checks on the identity of everybody seeking refugee status were not always very thorough, particularly for those who had already been given references by the Vatican. Nevertheless, it is difficult to avoid the conclusion that the Red Cross, one of the world's leading humanitarian organizations, at the very least colluded with those Catholic clerics who were helping Nazi war criminals escape justice.

THE SECRET ARCHIVES

Little doubt exists that some clerics stained the reputation of the Catholic Church by assisting Nazi war criminals, but it is far less clear how many people within the Church condoned what was happening. It has been alleged that Pope Pius XII, who reigned from 1939 until his death in 1958, must have at least been aware of the involvement of clerics like Bishop Hudal, not least because Hudal had been open about his Nazi sympathies before the war. Pius XII has also been criticized for not doing as much as he could have to oppose National Socialism during the war, though it should be remembered that any such action could have had serious repercussions for those Catholics living within the zone of Nazi occupation.

— ALTERNATIVE — THEORIES

On April 30, 1945, with the Soviet Red Army closing in on his air-raid shelter in Berlin, Adolf Hitler committed suicide along with Eva Braun, whom he had married two days previously. The two bodies were taken out of the subterranean bunker and placed in a shell hole, then doused in gasoline and burned. Rumors persist that the suicide never actually took place and that Hitler actually escaped to South America, where he is said to have lived in secret for several decades, protected by a core of diehard Nazis. No credible evidence exists to back up such claims, but, then again,

Above: Hitler meeting the Vatican ambassador to Germany. Could Hitler have used a ratline to escape to Argentina at the end of the Second World War?

no actual evidence that he died in the bunker, beyond the word of those who were there with him, exists either.

None of the documents held in the Vatican Secret Archives that relate to Pius XII are currently available for public viewing. It is customary for such papal archives to remain secret until seventy-five years after the pope's death. If this practice is followed for Pope Pius XII, we will have to wait until 2033 before finding out if the archive contains anything which will shed further light on what he knew about those of his clerics who helped Nazi war criminals. This level of secrecy may be normal practice, but it certainly adds to the impression that the Catholic Church has something to hide.

DID NASA FAKE THE MOON LANDINGS?

Date: 1969–1972
Location: USA and the moon

The moon landings are among humankind's greatest accomplishments, but some people believe that one of the great feats of the twentieth century never really happened.

Between 1969 and 1972, NASA's Apollo program landed a total of twelve astronauts on the moon in the course of six successful missions. On July 20, 1969, Neil Armstrong and Buzz Aldrin became the first men to walk on the moon, an event watched live on television by an estimated 600 million people. It was the culmination of many years of research and development by NASA, and represented an extraordinary milestone in human achievement. It also meant that the United States had comprehensively won the so-called "space race," an aspect of the Cold War with the Soviet Union in which the two opposing superpowers competed to outdo each other in advancing the technology of spaceflight. As well as the prestige attached to proving the superiority of the United States' technical ability, some saw victory in the space race as confirmation that capitalism and democracy would ultimately triumph over communism. It was also a demonstration that American rocket technology had surpassed the Soviet capability, including in its military applications, such as the delivery of ballistic missiles.

AN IMPOSSIBLE DREAM?

Up until the beginning of the Apollo program in the early 1960s, American research into spaceflight had been lagging behind the Soviet Union. The Soviet program had launched Sputnik, the first satellite, in 1957, and four years later, Yuri Gagarin became the first person to travel into space and complete an orbit of the Earth. The Soviet successes provoked a response from the United States, which included setting up NASA and initiating the Apollo program. In 1961, President John F. Kennedy made a speech committing the United States to "landing a man on the moon and returning him safely to Earth," before the end of the decade, giving NASA less than nine years to achieve the aim.

Above: Buzz Aldrin walking on the surface of the moon. Conspiracy theorists allege that photographs like this one were actually taken in a studio on Earth.

Kennedy's target was highly ambitious, given how far behind the Americans were, and, together with the American desire to win the space race, it has been cited by conspiracy theorists as being one of the principal reasons why the moon landings had to be faked. The technology available in the 1960s, they contend, was simply not advanced enough for a real moon landing to be possible, but NASA needed to show progress was being made to justify its multibillion-dollar budget. As getting a man to the moon and back could not be done, the only option, other than admitting that the feat was impossible, was to fake it.

Some conspiracy theorists have gone further, alleging that the government was also involved in the conspiracy because the

Above: A Soviet stamp celebrating Sputnik, the first satellite to orbit the Earth, which demonstrated the Soviet lead in the space race.

extraordinary achievement of landing a man on the moon would provide a distraction from the Vietnam War and the growing levels of civil disorder then occurring in the United States. It also provided an opportunity for fraud on an epic scale, because the billions of dollars of public money given to NASA could be channeled into companies with links to individuals in the government, in the form of lucrative contracts which did not have to be fulfilled.

It is, of course, easy to make accusations and rather harder to prove them. Most of the evidence used to support allegations that the moon landings were fake comes from interpretations of the film and still photographs of astronauts on the moon released by NASA, which, according to the conspiracy theorists, actually show that the pictures were really taken in a studio on Earth. Oft-cited examples are the lack of stars visible in any of the photographs and the fact that the U.S. flags planted on the moon appear to be fluttering in the wind; as there is no atmosphere on the moon, there could not have been any wind, so the flags should have been motionless. It has also been claimed that the angles of the shadows visible in many of the photographs show that multiple artificial light sources were being used, when the only light available on the moon would have been that from the sun.

THE EVIDENCE EXAMINED

One of the most convincing arguments against the faking of the moon landings is that it would have required an enormous and elaborate conspiracy involving many thousands of people in order for it to succeed. Even if it didn't unravel as it progressed, it would have been all but impossible to keep it secret. It is also hard to imagine that Neil Armstrong, Buzz Aldrin, and the other astronauts involved spent their entire lives lying about what they had achieved, or that not one of the scientists and technicians involved in the mission, who must have known if it was fake, has ever admitted it.

The evidence put forward by conspiracy theorists has also been thoroughly debunked. The flagpoles used on the moon, for instance, were designed with a metal bar running along the top of the flag to hold it out because NASA was well aware of the lack of wind on the moon. Had a normal flagpole been used, the flag would have hung limply against the pole so that the Stars and Stripes would not have been visible. All the photographs were taken during the lunar day, when there was enough available light, so, just as on Earth, no stars were visible. The multiple shadows in the photographs could have been caused by light reflecting from the surface of the moon or off the lunar module, while the amount

Right: The Apollo 11 astronauts who made the first manned moon landing. From left, Neil Armstrong, Michael Collins, and Buzz Aldrin.

Left: An American flag on the moon. A metal rod running along the top of the flag ensures that it does not hang limply against the pole.

of lunar dust in the air would have had the effect of diffusing light from the sun, making it difficult to know for certain which direction shadows would have fallen in.

In truth, all the supposed photographic evidence of a conspiracy has been easily dismissed and, in any case, it has been demonstrated that the rocks brought back from the moon could not have come from anywhere else. The missions were tracked by a number of different countries, including the Soviet Union, without any reports of anything suspicious occurring, while lunar probes sent up by, among others, China and India have detected the landing sites of the Apollo lunar modules and the debris left behind. Needless to say, all of this has not been enough to change the minds of diehard conspiracy theorists. But in order to convince the rest of us that NASA really did fake the moon landings, and have been fooling us ever since, they will have to come up with much better evidence than they have done so far.

— ALTERNATIVE —
THEORIES

One of the known hazards of flying into space from the Earth is exposure to increased levels of radiation once a spacecraft has traveled beyond the magnetosphere, which is the extent to which the Earth's magnetic field stretches out into space. The radiation is mostly caused by charged particles emitted from the Sun during solar flares, then carried toward the Earth by solar wind, and is also present in cosmic rays from outside our solar system. The magnetic field forms a shield around the Earth, protecting us from the harmful effects of the radiation as the charged particles in solar wind and cosmic rays are either deflected away or held in the magnetosphere to form what are known as Van Allen belts.

In order to get to the moon, the Apollo missions had to travel through both the inner and outer Van Allen belts, which, according to some conspiracy theories, would have exposed astronauts to lethal doses of radiation, thereby making manned moon landings impossible.

Above: An illustration showing how the Earth's magnetic field shields the planet from charged particles in solar wind to form Van Allen belts.

NASA has countered these accusations by showing how it calculated the trajectories of the spacecraft to minimize exposure to the most intense regions of radiation within the Van Allen belts. The Apollo spacecraft actually passed through the belts quickly enough that the astronauts received very low doses of radiation, well within the limits considered safe for people who work in the nuclear energy industry. Radiation remains a problem for any proposed space travel, but does not appear to be an insurmountable one.

HAS FEMA BUILT A SECRET NETWORK OF CONCENTRATION CAMPS?

Date: 1979 onwards
Location: USA

Some believe the real function of the Federal Emergency Management Agency (FEMA) is not to protect U.S. citizens in case of disaster, but to intern them in concentration camps.

The conspiracy theories concerning FEMA share a common thread of anti-government paranoia. They envisage a time when a U.S. president will use the executive powers of the office to suspend the constitution and declare martial law. Hundreds of thousands, if not millions, of Americans will then be rounded up and sent to concentration camps constructed in secret by FEMA. There, they will either be permanently incarcerated or exterminated while a totalitarian government is installed. The identities of the people to be interned or murdered vary from one version of the theory to another. However, it's often said that the camps will target those who are right-wing and conservative in their political outlook, such as gun owners, anti-abortionists, survivalists, Evangelical Christians, and members of the alt-right.

Above: The only FEMA camps that have so far come to light are those used for disaster relief work, such as this one in Beaumont, Texas.

THE RISE OF THE THEORY

FEMA was originally set up in 1979 to provide a coordinated federal response to national disasters such as major hurricanes. Soon after its inception, conspiracy theorists began to allege that this stated purpose was actually a cover story for its real, more sinister, aim: to set up a network of concentration camps across the United States where the government could imprison all those people it considered to be undesirable. At first these claims were widely dismissed, but over the years they have come to be accepted by an increasingly large number of people.

After Barack Obama was elected to the presidency in 2009, elements in the right-wing media began to promote the FEMA camps theory—along with a range of other stories concerning Obama's origins and religious affiliations—and this attention brought the possibility of the existence of such camps into the mainstream. As well as being discussed by TV presenters and radio talk show hosts, the theory was mentioned by several Republican Party politicians, including Donald Trump, giving it greater credibility than it had previously enjoyed. Even so, it is hard to believe that many Americans really believed they were in imminent danger of being rounded up and thrown into concentration camps.

CAMPS AND COFFINS

It is, of course, one thing to make these allegations and entirely another to provide evidence to back up the claims. Most of the evidence produced in support of the FEMA camps theory has been photographic, but to date all the images purporting to show the camps have been exposed as fake. For instance, an aerial photograph said to show a secret prison facility in Wyoming proved, on closer inspection, to be a forced labor camp in North Korea. Other supposed FEMA camps have turned out to be a National Guard training center and a facility used by Amtrak to maintain its trains.

Another line of evidence used in support of the FEMA camps theory is the claim that, shortly after being elected, Obama placed an order for 500,000 plastic coffins, apparently to be used to bury the bodies of those exterminated in the camps. Photographs appeared on the internet of a site near Atlanta, Georgia, where thousands of coffin-sized black plastic containers were piled up. Rather than being coffins for murdered Americans, however, a more straightforward explanation quickly emerged. The containers were in fact burial vaults, manufactured and stored at the site by a company based in Georgia. The plastic containers are commonly used when a coffin is interred in a cemetary, to prevent earth from collapsing in on it.

So far, no network of concentration camps has come to light, but, if the theory is correct, then this network would have to be extensive enough to incarcerate millions of people. Such an enormous project would require a large workforce to construct the camps and trained staff to deal with detainees once martial law has been declared. Keeping all these camps hidden and maintaining secrecy among the thousands of people involved in setting up and running them would present FEMA with an enormous challenge (one which, given the organization's record in disaster relief, it doesn't give the impression of being capable of meeting).

— ALTERNATIVE —
THEORIES

The peaceful handover of power that occurred between President Obama and President Trump in January 2017 should, it may be thought, have put an end to the FEMA camps stories. But conspiracy theories have a tendency to evolve with the times, and, rather than admitting they were wrong, proponents have adapted to meet the new circumstances. Some now claim that President Trump has been kept in the dark about the conspiracy and those members of the liberal elite who are behind it are waiting for the right moment to remove him from power. Once this has been

Above: Conspiracy theorists believe that the true nature of FEMA has been kept secret from President Trump.

achieved, martial law will be declared, detentions will begin, and the camps will fill up with American citizens.

Despite the complete lack of credible evidence, the conspiracy theories continued throughout Obama's presidency. A large number of Americans appeared to distrust their government to such an extent that they believed it was capable of committing genocidal acts on the scale of those perpetrated by the Nazis in Germany during the Second World War. This extraordinary level of mistrust may, in some part at least, account for the level of support received by Donald Trump during the 2016 presidential election. Perhaps it also indicates the potential influence of conspiracy theories once they are believed by a significant number of people.

WHO KNEW ABOUT THE IRAN–CONTRA AFFAIR?

Date: 1985–1987
Location: USA

As the Iran-Contra affair unfolded in 1986, senior figures in the administration of President Ronald Reagan were implicated, but it is still unclear how much the president himself knew.

The scandal had its roots in the foreign policies pursued by the Reagan administration and the constraints on what a U.S. president can do without the support of Congress. The affair involved a complicated conspiracy to use the profits made from secret arms sales to Iran to support Contra rebels in Nicaragua, who were engaged in a guerrilla war against the socialist government of the Sandinistas. Arms sales to Iran were subject to an embargo imposed by President Jimmy Carter in 1979, and funding the Contras was prohibited by the Boland Amendment, part of a bill passed in 1984 by both houses of Congress. The scandal also raised constitutional issues, because non-elected officials had secretly conducted foreign policy without the oversight of elected members of Congress. Everything that happened in the administration was ultimately the responsibility of the president and, if Reagan had authorized or even known about what had been happening, then he had acted both illegally and unconstitutionally.

Right: Contra guerrillas in Nicaragua. The Contras were funded by the United States to oppose the democratically elected socialist Sandinista government.

THE REAGAN DOCTRINE

The connection between Iran and Nicaragua, at least as far as U.S. foreign policy was concerned, was that revolutions in both countries had removed regimes backed by the United States, leading to closer ties with the Soviet Union. The United States' principal foreign policy strategy was the so-called Reagan Doctrine, which involved instituting measures to "roll back" the influence of the Soviet Union around the world, by opposing communist and left-wing governments.

Iran was fighting a costly war with Iraq at that time and, with the American embargo in place, had turned to the Soviet Union to buy military equipment. The secret arms deal proposed by the Reagan administration was an attempt to reduce Iran's reliance on the Soviet Union and also to induce the Iranian government to use its influence with the Lebanese militant group Hezbollah to secure the release of seven American hostages they were holding. Arms shipments began in 1985, initially going through Israel until a modification to the plan was proposed by Oliver North, who would become a central figure in the unfolding scandal. North was

Above: President Reagan (right) in the Oval Office of the White House with his aides Casper Weinberger, George Shultz, Ed Meese, and Don Regan.

a colonel in the U.S. Marines who was acting as an aide to the National Security Council (NSC), the body charged with advising the president on foreign policy and security. It was North who suggested selling arms directly to Iran and using the profits to secretly fund the Contras.

The Contras had been fighting against the Nicaraguan government since 1979, when the Sandinistas had overthrown the American-backed dictatorship of President Anastasio Somoza Debayle. On gaining power, the Sandinistas had initiated a range of socialist policies, including the nationalization of big companies and the redistribution of land from wealthy landowners to poor people. In an effort to prevent the spread of socialism further across Central America, the Reagan administration funded the Contras, despite the knowledge that they were involved in drug trafficking and had committed numerous acts of terrorism. After Congress had passed the Boland Amendment, the funding should have stopped and, without U.S. support, the Contras might have faded into insignificance. North's plan of secretly channeling money from Iranian arms sales to the Contras allowed them to keep fighting, so the policies of the Reagan Doctrine continued to be implemented in Nicaragua even though the method by which this was achieved was clearly illegal.

A SHREDDING PARTY

On October 5, 1986, a plane was shot down over Nicaragua while transporting arms and supplies to the Contras. The only survivor was an American citizen, while the plane was registered to a cargo company with links to the CIA. A month later, reports appeared in a Lebanese newspaper giving details of the arms for hostages deal between the United States and Iran, the information apparently leaked from within Iran's Revolutionary Guard. The Iranian government confirmed the reports, and President Reagan appeared on TV to defend the actions of his administration as being a means of securing the release of American hostages.

It had become clear that the NSC was directly involved and had surpassed its role as an advisory body, leading to an investigation by the office of the U.S. attorney general. On November 21, the day before his office was due to be searched, Oliver North and his secretary, Fawn Hall, held what he later described as a "shredding party," in which numerous documents relating to the affair were destroyed. One crucial document escaped the shredder, however, and provided investigators with details of the connection between arms sales to Iran and funding for the Contras.

Below: The mugshot of Oliver North taken after he was arrested and charged with sixteen felonies relating to his role in the Iran–Contra Affair.

The discovery of the Diversion Memo, as it became known, led to President Reagan sacking North and to Admiral John Poindexter, the head of the NSC, resigning. It was subsequently claimed that knowledge of the affair had not gone any higher than Poindexter, however unlikely it might seem that he would have engaged in such activities without seeking authorization from above. Two inquires were conducted into the affair, one appointed by the president and the other commissioned by Congress. Having previously denied that the United States would do deals with terrorists or hostage-takers, Reagan was forced to admit that he had known about the arms deal with Iran, but maintained he knew nothing about the diversion of funds to the Contras.

OLIVER L NORTH
DOB 10 7 43

Both inquires were critical of the president's conduct, particularly in allowing the NSC to

Above: Iranians celebrating the Islamic Revolution, which ousted the U.S.-backed Shah and led to a break in diplomatic relations with the United States.

conduct its own operations without oversight, but they did not find evidence that he had known the full extent of what had occurred. The congressional committee made the point that it was his responsibility to have known and also stated that it had not been possible to establish the full extent of the illegality because so many documents had been shredded. Oliver North would later write that he had kept President Reagan informed about every step of the operation with regular briefings, but no evidence has survived to substantiate these claims.

In all, fourteen people were charged with offenses relating to the scandal, including Oliver North and John Poindexter. Most of the charges were relatively minor and, of the eleven who were convicted, all those who did not have their convictions overturned on appeal were later given presidential pardons by George H. W. Bush, who had been vice-president during the scandal. Now, more than thirty years later, it still remains unclear exactly what President Reagan knew about the affair or if he had authorized any of the illegal activity himself. Many Americans have given him the benefit of the doubt, even though, in a country that upholds the rule of law, everybody should be held accountable for their actions, no matter who they are or what public office they hold.

— ALTERNATIVE —
THEORIES

When the Iran–Contra affair first came to light, allegations were made that the CIA not only knew about the involvement of the Contras in drug trafficking but had facilitated it. It was implied that the same routes employed to airlift arms to Nicaragua were being used to bring cocaine back into the United States, and the profits from this trade were funding the Contras. A congressional committee chaired by Senator John Kerry in April 1989 reported that some elements within the Contras had been involved in trafficking, but did not find anything to connect them to the CIA.

Above: Bags of cocaine: Gary Webb alleged that the CIA was involved in trafficking the drug into the United States to support the Contras.

In 1996, a series of articles by the investigative reporter Gary Webb, published in the San Jose *Mercury News*, claimed to have uncovered the principal route used by the traffickers and alleged that the CIA had been largely responsible for starting the crack cocaine epidemic that had afflicted Los Angeles, California, at that time. The articles pointed toward CIA involvement in the trafficking, prompting a number of investigations by other newspapers, including the *Washington Post* and *New York Times*, and by several federal agencies, all of which concluded that Webb had exaggerated the impact of the cocaine trafficking, finding no evidence of a link to the CIA. Webb contended that the mainstream media had been manipulated by the government and CIA to discredit his story. In 2004, he was found dead at his home with two gunshot wounds to his head. The local coroner's office ruled that he had died by suicide.

WAS HIV CREATED IN A LABORATORY?

Date: 1980s
Location: USA

Ever since HIV was identified as the cause of AIDS, some conspiracy theorists have claimed that the virus was created as a biological weapon and a despicable means of control.

A cure for HIV has yet to be found, but in recent years treatment has advanced to the point where it can be controlled with antiretroviral drugs so that the symptoms of AIDS do not develop. In countries where such treatment is available, people who are HIV-positive can now expect to live relatively normal lives and have an average life expectancy approaching that of people who do not have the virus. This was very far from the case in 1981, when AIDS was first clinically observed in the United States. Then, an increasing number of people, many of them gay men, had developed a range of symptoms caused by the suppression of their immune systems; this left them vulnerable to secondary infections, which ultimately led to their deaths. HIV was first proposed as being the cause of AIDS in 1983; once this had been established, it allowed medical science to begin the development of treatments and the search for a cure. The apparently sudden appearance of AIDS among the gay community led to questions about where the disease had come from in the first place. Medical science had a theory to explain its origin, but others came to different conclusions.

THE AIDS EPIDEMIC

According to medical science, HIV evolved in Central Africa, where at some point in the 1920s a similar virus which infected chimpanzees had mutated, allowing it to cross the species barrier into humans. It then spread slowly to other parts of Africa and further afield, but was not recognized as a specific disease until clusters of gay men with similar symptoms came to the notice of doctors in the United States. It took a long time for the disease to be recognized because it can take ten years or more for HIV infections to develop into AIDS and because, once the disease has developed, death is caused by secondary infections, such as pneumonia or tuberculosis, rather than by the virus itself.

While the cause of AIDS remained unknown, space existed for all sorts of explanations of its origins to arise which had little to do with medical science. According to some evangelical Christian

Right: Two men at the New York Gay Pride parade in June 1984. At that time, HIV had only just been discovered to be the cause of AIDS.

groups, AIDS was God's punishment for homosexuality, while others contended that it was not a disease at all. People who had died of AIDS, they argued, had done so because their lifestyle choices had damaged their immune systems, not because they had contracted a disease. Such opinions persisted long after it had become clear that HIV caused AIDS, demonstrating that these views were based more on prejudice against those minority groups most at risk from the disease than on any sort of reasoned argument.

HIV AS A BIOWEAPON

Most conspiracy theories accept that HIV is the cause of AIDS, but allege that it was developed as a bioweapon to control the populations of certain groups of people. A disproportionately high number of African Americans have contracted HIV, leading to speculation that the virus was intentionally designed as a means of reducing or eliminating the population of black people in the United States. A similar theory exists in those parts of Africa where HIV rates are highest, except this time it is seen as a Western attempt to wipe out black Africans in order to take control of the natural resources of the continent. The high incidence of HIV among gay men, who could be from any race, has been explained away as the result of tests conducted by the U.S. government on what was considered to be another "undesirable" minority group.

One argument against these theories is that the nature of HIV makes it highly ineffective as a bioweapon because it exhibits exactly the opposite characteristics to those required. It can be contracted by anybody rather than afflicting a particular race or group, it spreads slowly and only under a particular set of circumstances, and it takes years before it progresses to the point of being fatal. In truth, it should hardly be necessary to raise such objections because the theories have all been comprehensively discredited by medical science. Even so, some have proved persistent, and these can have dangerous consequences. One theory, for instance, suggests that HIV was intentionally spread

— ALTERNATIVE —
THEORIES

In 1985, the KGB began a campaign of disinformation known as Operation INFEKTION, which was aimed at increasing anti-American feeling around the world. Through articles placed in newspapers in the Soviet Union and other communist countries, INFEKTION attempted to spread rumors that HIV had been created in the U.S. Army's former biological weapons research facility at Fort Detrick in Maryland. The articles reported the research of Jakob Segal, a professor of biology at an East German university, who claimed that HIV had been made by splicing together two other viruses. Despite his research being completely discredited, the Soviet

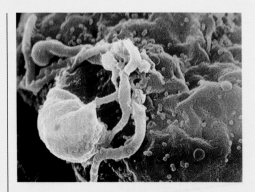

Above: An enhanced image from a scanning electron micrograph showing the human immunodeficiency virus in the process of budding.

campaign to publicize it may well have played a role in the proliferation of the conspiracy theories which continue to be repeated today.

in Africa through programs to vaccinate against a variety of infectious diseases. If believed, such a theory could result in people being put at risk from those diseases because they are afraid of being vaccinated against them. This demonstrates that, while the majority of fabricated conspiracy theories are essentially harmless, those concerning the origin of HIV, which have no substance to them at all, can be very damaging and even have the potential to cause unnecessary deaths.

POLITICAL CONSPIRACIES

T he old joke that we can always tell when politicians are lying to us because we can see their lips moving is funny because we all recognize an element of truth in it. It is a sign of an erosion of trust in politicians which, given the dirty tricks some have gotten up to, is hardly a surprise. In this section, we deal with some of the underhand schemes politicians have attempted to get away with over the years, including those perpetrated by the man considered by many to be the dirtiest of them all, President Richard Nixon, or Tricky Dicky, as he was otherwise known.

Nixon was brought down by the Watergate scandal, specifically by his attempts to

obstruct investigations into it, and here we deal with one of the aspects of the affair which remains unsolved: the original purpose of the burglary committed at the Watergate Complex in Washington, D.C., which ignited the scandal. As well as looking at politicians, we also consider a number of conspiracy theories that have alleged the involvement of organizations like the Illuminati and the Bilderberg Group in secret plots to manipulate political systems around the world, and we examine the conspiracy of denial that continues today in Turkey over the Armenian Genocide. While idealistic politicians who want to make the world a better place may actually exist, the ones we cover here do not fall into that category, and knowledge of what they have done is unlikely to restore our faith in our leaders.

Left: Richard Nixon celebrating in 1972, shortly before the Watergate scandal broke.

DID THE POPE AND THE KING CONSPIRE TO DESTROY THE KNIGHTS TEMPLAR?

Date: 1307–14
Location: France

In 1307, hundreds of Knights Templar were arrested by King Philip IV of France. What we don't know is whether he conspired with the Pope to destroy the order.

The Knights Templar was founded as a Catholic military order in about 1119 in Jerusalem. It was formed in the aftermath of the First Crusade, during which the city had been seized from its Islamic rulers. The Knights' original purpose was to protect Christian pilgrims making the dangerous journey from Europe to the Holy Land, and the order grew rich from gifts of land, property, and money from wealthy benefactors. It also benefited from being granted special status by the Pope, placing it under the sole authority of the papacy and exempting its members from the laws and taxes of the countries where they lived. After much of the Holy Land was retaken by the Islamic forces of Saladin in the late twelfth century, the Templars' role as the protectors of pilgrims declined, but by that time they had diversified into a wide range of business activities, including an

Right: A painting depicting the Knights Templar attacking Jerusalem in 1299. In reality, by then they were more businessmen than crusaders.

early form of banking, and their wealth continued to grow. More than a hundred years later, they became the target of King Philip IV of France, who had borrowed a great deal of money from the order and was not inclined to pay it back.

PHILIP'S DEBTS

The debts Philip had incurred were due to the numerous wars he had fought since gaining the throne in 1285, principally against King Edward I of England. In 1296, he attempted to raise money by imposing taxes on the clergy in France, a move resisted by Pope Boniface VIII, who issued a number of decrees aimed at maintaining the supreme position of the papacy above any secular rulers. It was the start of a long-running dispute between the two, which would only come to an end in 1303 with Boniface's death.

In other efforts to raise money, Philip expelled Lombard merchants and Jews from France and seized their assets, but he did not have authority to move against the wealthiest group in the country, the Knights Templar, because they answered only to the authority of the pope. After the death of Pope Boniface, and as a means of achieving his apparent aim of destroying the Templars, Philip is thought by some historians to have initiated a plan to install a pope who was

Above: A late fourteenth-century illustration of Jacques de Molay, the last Grandmaster of the Knights Templar, being burned at the stake with a fellow Knight.

more amenable to his wishes. The pope who succeeded Boniface, Benedict XI, died after only eight months in office and, while we don't know the exact circumstances, it has been alleged that he was poisoned by Guillaume de Nogaret, one of Philip's most trusted ministers. After Benedict's sudden death, he was followed by Pope Clement V, who, unlike his two Italian predecessors, was French. We don't know if there was a secret agreement in which Philip supported Clement's candidacy, but one of the first things Clement did on being elected was to move the seat of the papacy from Rome to Avignon, a free city in the Holy Roman Empire, surrounded by French territory; this placed it within Philip's sphere of influence.

THE KING AND THE POPE

Almost as soon as Clement had become Pope in 1305, Philip accused the Templars of committing a long list of crimes, principal among these being the charge of heresy. Clement insisted on following proper procedure by conducting full investigations of the charges, and by Friday October 13, 1307, the delay this caused appears to have prompted Philip to take the matter into his own hands by arresting large numbers of Templars. Confessions of heresy were extracted under torture from many of those arrested and some were then burned at the stake before trials could be held. Shortly afterward, Clement gave his support to Philip's actions by issuing a papal decree ordering all the Christians monarchs of Europe to arrest every Templar within their territory and seize their property.

Philip's efforts dragged on over the course of the next five years, until, in 1312, the Templar order was officially abolished by a papal decree issued by Clement at the Council of Vienne. Two years later, the last Grand Master of the Templars, Jacques de Molay,

— ALTERNATIVE —
THEORIES

S ome speculate that Philip's reason for destroying the Templars may not have been to avoid paying his debts, but to further his ambition of becoming the supreme power in France. To achieve this aim, he conspired to install a pope he could control, thereby effectively making himself the religious leader of France as well as its king. With Clement in his pocket, Philip then destroyed the Templars because the order was not under his authority and, as such, represented a threat to him. Rather than being about money, then, Philip's actions could ultimately have been concerned with building a French state which fell completely under his power.

Above: Pope Clement V. Philip may have helped Clement become pope on the condition that he then aided the king in destroying the Templars.

was arrested, put on trial, and then burned at the stake, leaving no doubt that Philip had fully achieved his aim. Now, more than seven hundred years later, it is impossible to be certain that Philip and Clement colluded together to destroy the Templars, even if it is hard to believe that Philip could have achieved his aims so successfully without Clement's support. But, however it was achieved, by 1314 the Knights Templar had effectively ceased to exist.

WHO WAS BEHIND THE GUNPOWDER PLOT?

Date: November 5, 1605
Location: London, England

The Gunpowder Plot was an attempt by Catholics to assassinate the Protestant King James I, but some historians believe it was part of a deeper conspiracy conceived by the English government.

Guy Fawkes was discovered with thirty-six barrels of gunpowder in the cellars of the House of Lords in London on November 5, 1605. It was the night before the State Opening of Parliament, which King James I was due to attend. The story is very well known in Britain, where it is remembered every year on Bonfire Night, November 5, even if the religious aspects of the plot have long since faded from the collective memory.

Catholics had been persecuted in England since the beginning of the Protestant Reformation in the 1530s, and numerous plots had been attempted by recusants, those Catholics who refused to convert, aimed at replacing the reigning Protestant monarch with one who was either Catholic or at least sympathetic toward the Roman Church. The aim of the Gunpowder Plot was to kill King James, together with most of the members of his government,

and replace him with his nine-year-old daughter Elizabeth, who, the plotters thought, could be manipulated into returning England to Catholicism.

The scheme was led by Robert Catesby, who came from a prominent Catholic family in Warwickshire. The exact circumstances which led Catesby to initiate a plot to kill King James are not known, but some time in early 1604 he began to enlist young Catholic men to take part. His recruits included Thomas Percy, Francis Tresham, and around ten others. Guy Fawkes, the man now most associated with the plot, was recruited in the Netherlands, where he was fighting for the Catholics in a religious war between Catholic and Protestant forces. He was a valuable asset to the conspirators, because his military career had provided him with the experience needed to handle the explosives they intended to use.

Above: Bonfire Night— in Britain, the failure of the Gunpowder Plot is still celebrated with fireworks and the burning of an effigy of Guy Fawkes.

THE PLOT UNRAVELS
In the months leading up to the State Opening of Parliament, the plotters rented cellars underneath the House of Lords, where they stored barrels of gunpowder concealed under firewood.

Above: A 1605 engraving of eight of the conspirators, by Crispijn van de Passe. Guy Fawkes is third from the right, between Percy and Catesby.

But, unknown to the plotters, their plan had been compromised. On October 26, the Catholic peer Lord Monteagle was sent an anonymous letter warning him not to attend parliament because it would "receive a terrible blow," and suggested that, for the good of his health, he should make an excuse and retire to the country.

Monteagle showed the letter to Robert Cecil, the secretary of state in the English government. Little appears to have been done about it until November 4, when a search of the Houses of Parliament was conducted. Fawkes, who had been given the job of lighting the fuse, was discovered in the cellar with the firewood. He claimed to be a servant of Thomas Percy by the name of John Johnson and was allowed to leave. In the early hours of the following day, the king ordered a second search and this time it was carried out more thoroughly. Fawkes was again found in the cellar and the pile of firewood was investigated, uncovering the gunpowder. Fawkes was arrested, still claiming to be John Johnson, and for several days refused to reveal anything about the plot even though he was subjected to torture. The remaining plotters all escaped from London, but were either caught or killed over the course of the next few days. Catesby and Percy were both shot dead after being discovered in a house in Staffordshire, and the remaining plotters were put on trial for treason, found guilty, and executed, with the exception of Tresham, who had died from an infection before standing trial.

AN INSIDE JOB?

No evidence exists to show that the plot to kill the king was anything other than a conspiracy among a group of disgruntled Catholics, but there are grounds to speculate that there could have been more to it than meets the eye. The focus of

Above: A detail of an 1823 painting by Henry Perronet Briggs, which depicts the moment Guy Fawkes is discovered in the cellar and the plot is foiled.

the speculation has been Robert Cecil, who was virulently anti-Catholic and, at least according to one theory, may have been alarmed by the greater level of tolerance James exhibited toward Catholics than his predecessor, Queen Elizabeth I, had shown. If this was the case, then perhaps Cecil instigated the Gunpowder Plot to demonstrate to James the threat posed by Catholics, in the expectation that it would induce him to become much more staunchly anti-Catholic.

Such underhand methods were known to have been used at that time. In 1586, for example, the Babington Plot, a Catholic conspiracy to assassinate Elizabeth and replace her with Mary, Queen of Scots, was infiltrated and manipulated by government spies. Mary was trapped into giving her ascent to the plot, an act of treason which led to her execution. Lord Burghley, Cecil's father, was one of Elizabeth's closest advisers and had been involved in the plot along with Sir Francis Walsingham, her secretary of state, who is often referred to as Elizabeth's spymaster. Could Cecil have employed similar methods to infiltrate the

Gunpowder Plot and turn it to his advantage, or could he even have been behind it right from the beginning?

At the heart of the matter is the anonymous letter sent to Lord Monteagle. It was clearly written by somebody with knowledge of the plot and has often been attributed to Francis Tresham, who was Monteagle's brother-in-law. But could it have been written by Cecil or somebody in his employ to provide him with the means of exposing the plot without revealing that he had been behind it? The length of time between Monteagle receiving the letter, on October 26, and the first search of the Houses of Parliament on November 4 certainly suggests something rather strange was going on; otherwise, why was the search not conducted straight away? If Cecil really was attempting to persuade James of the threat posed by Catholics, perhaps he waited until a few hours before the State Opening of Parliament before revealing the plot to ensure that James realized the immediacy of the danger he was in.

An obvious reason to suppose that the plot was not a government inside job is that, if it was Cecil, he had taken an enormous risk by allowing such a large quantity of gunpowder to be hidden under the House of Lords for a period of several months. The fact that the plot got as close as it did to killing James was also deeply embarrassing for the government, and particularly for Cecil, because it exposed the vulnerability of the king and demonstrated that the government could not be relied on to protect him. If Cecil really was behind the scheme, then maintaining secrecy would have been paramount because, if his involvement had been discovered, he would most likely have joined Fawkes and the other plotters at the executioner's block. In the event, James did not crack down on Catholics in the aftermath of the failed plot, so, even if Cecil was involved, his supposed plan to force the king to become more anti-Catholic did not succeed. Equally, if this was the case, his efforts to maintain secrecy certainly worked, and today we remain uncertain of any role he may have played.

— ALTERNATIVE —
THEORIES

The Gunpowder Plot could have been a government setup right from the start, devised by Cecil as a means of ensnaring those recusants who could be tempted into committing treason by the prospect of England becoming a Catholic country once again. There are some indications, though no absolute proof, that Robert Catesby met with Cecil on a number of occasions as the plot developed, and Thomas Percy is known to have had connections inside the government, which he used to secure the lease on the cellars underneath the House of Lords where the barrels of gunpowder were placed. Could Catesby and Percy, either individually or in collusion, have being working for Cecil as anti-Catholic agents right from the beginning?

Catesby and Percy were the only two of the plotters to be killed before being captured, leading to suggestions that Cecil did not want either of them taken alive in case they revealed his involvement in the plot. If this

Above: Could Robert Cecil, secretary of state in James I's government, have conceived the plot as a way of stirring up anti-Catholic sentiment?

was the case, then, before they were betrayed by Cecil themselves, Catesby and Percy had intentionally set up Fawkes and the others as fall guys in the certain knowledge that, once the plot was exposed, all of them would be executed. No evidence has ever come to light to support such a theory and most historians of the period do not accept it, instead taking the Gunpowder Plot at face value: a genuine Catholic conspiracy to kill the king.

DO THE ILLUMINATI STILL EXIST?

Date: 1776… until today?
Location: Bavaria

Some conspiracy theorists believe that the Illuminati, a secret society founded in Bavaria in 1776, have been behind almost every major event in world history ever since.

The Illuminati, which means "the Enlightened Ones," were disbanded after less than ten years, being considered subversive by the Bavarian authorities and the Catholic Church. Their original purpose was to spread the ideals of the Enlightenment, of reason and rational thinking above belief and superstition. In this day and age, such aims may not appear very radical, but Bavaria was staunchly Catholic in the late eighteenth century, so the founding members may have decided to keep their activities to themselves so as not to attract the attention of anybody in authority. Alternatively, as most of the early members had been involved with the Freemasons, perhaps they simply preferred the idea of a secret society because it gave the impression they were involved in clandestine activity. Whatever the case, the secrecy surrounding the identity of the membership and their activities would later lead to the Illuminati becoming the focus of numerous theories concerning members' supposed plans to take over the world. Many of these theories give the impression of being works of fantasy, but could any of them have some basis in reality?

THE ENLIGHTENED ONES

The organization was founded by the philosopher Adam Weishaupt in the Bavarian city of Ingolstadt. From an original membership of four, the society slowly grew and spread to other Bavarian cities, recruiting its members largely through contacts in the Freemasons. Members assumed aliases and the society adopted secret signs and ceremonies in the same way as the Freemasons had, though it is not clear if they actually did very much other than hold meetings and talk about their ideals.

Above: A contemporary engraving of Adam Weishaupt, the philosopher from Ingolstadt who founded the original Illuminati.

Many of the first recruits were students, but by 1784 membership had broadened to include older and more influential men. The number of members had increased to somewhere in the region of a thousand, and branches had been started in Munich, Berlin, and Vienna. The society had become powerful enough to attract the attention of Church leaders, who were alarmed by its anti-religious nature. They persuaded Charles Theodore, the Elector of Bavaria, to take action and, in 1785, he issued an order banning all secret societies. Written documents and pamphlets produced by the Illuminati were seized and declared to be seditious, and Weishaupt fled Bavaria before he could be arrested. The society's branches disbanded and appears to have effectively ceased to exist.

A NEW WORLD ORDER

In 1797, books written by Augustin Barruel and John Robison, separately, made allegations that the Illuminati had not disbanded, its members having instead infiltrated the Freemasons as a means of gaining influence so that they could continue to disseminate their ideas. They claimed that the Illuminati had been secretly behind the French Revolution which had overthrown the *Ancien Régime* in 1789 and established France as a republic. In common with many modern conspiracy theorists, Barruel and Robison did not offer any corroborating evidence to back up their allegations, instead relying on speculation and innuendo. Nevertheless, their books were widely read and can now be regarded as the starting point for the numerous conspiracies relating to the Illuminati which developed in the latter half of the twentieth century.

Rather than being a secret society dedicated to spreading the ideals of the Enlightenment, more recent conspiracy theorists usually depict the modern incarnation of the Illuminati as a clique of the super-rich and powerful who aim to control the world's political and financial institutions. Their ultimate purpose is supposedly to establish a so-called New World Order, a global government run by the world's elite. In some versions of this theory, the modern Illuminati are said to be the direct descendants of the original Bavarian society, while in others the two are not related. The Illuminati and the New World Order have also been conflated with a supposed plot by Jewish bankers to take over the world, in conspiracies constructed by anti-semitic theorists, but these reflect their own prejudices rather than reality.

It is not made clear in any of the conspiracy theories why a modern secret society with its eyes on global domination would model itself on the Bavarian Illuminati, given that

Below: A French illustration from 1867 of an Illuminati initiation ceremony. The society's members were alleged to have been behind the French Revolution.

— ALTERNATIVE —
THEORIES

Skull and Bones is an undergraduate senior secret society at Yale University which has featured in some conspiracy theories as being an American branch of the Illuminati. It was first established in 1832 and former Bonesmen, as its members are known, have included numerous influential politicians and businessmen—members of the "power elite." In 2004, for instance, both the Republican and Democratic candidates in the U.S. presidential election, George W. Bush and John Kerry, were Bonesmen. No connection with the Illuminati has ever

Above: A group portrait of Bonesmen from 1904, posed with human bones on a table. Members have included notable politicians and businessmen.

been established, but then again, it is a secret society so, even if there was, the Bonesmen wouldn't tell us.

the intentions of the two would appear to be completely at odds. Rather than spreading Enlightenment ideas, the modern Illuminati are said to be attempting to impose a New World Order against the will of the people, creating what would essentially be a global fascist state. There may well be people in the world today who consider themselves to be part of a global elite and who would be prepared to go to any lengths necessary to maintain their self-appointed status. But there is no genuine indication that these people have anything to do with an eighteenth-century Bavarian secret society, or even that the Illuminati survived in any form at all beyond the 1780s, let alone into modern times.

DID THE OTTOMAN GOVERNMENT SANCTION THE ARMENIAN GENOCIDE?

Date: 1915

Location: The Ottoman Empire (modern-day Turkey)

The Armenian Genocide remains a sensitive subject in Turkey today, with the Turkish government refusing to recognize the events as genocide and attempting to silence those who do.

During the First World War, the territory the Armenians regarded as their homeland, in Eastern Anatolia and the Caucasus, was split between two of the protagonists. On one side was the Ottoman Empire, which had joined with Germany and Austria-Hungary, and on the other was the Russian Empire, allied to Britain and France. Russia held long-standing ambitions to expand its empire into Anatolia, with the ultimate goal of capturing Constantinople, as Istanbul was then called, and controlling the Bosphorus, the narrow strait joining the Mediterranean Sea with the Black Sea. By doing so, Russia could guarantee access to its only warm-water ports, on the Black Sea coast in Ukraine and Crimea. The Ottomans, meanwhile, wanted to recapture territory in the Caucasus region that they had lost to Russia in previous wars. Fighting between the two

Right: Ottoman soldiers in April 1915 marching Armenian civilians out of the town of Harput in Eastern Anatolia to a prison camp.

empires occurred in Eastern Anatolia, the region of the Armenian homeland within the Ottoman Empire, and it was against this background that the genocide of Armenian civilians occurred.

THE ARMENIANS AND THE OTTOMANS

The Armenians living within the Ottoman Empire constituted a Christian minority within an overwhelmingly Islamic state. On the whole, the Ottomans were reasonably tolerant of religious minorities, but were suspicious of the Armenians living near the border with Russia because of their shared Christian faith. In December 1914, the Ottoman Army, under the direct command of Enver Pasha, the minister of war, suffered a humiliating defeat by the Russians at the Battle of Sarikamish in Eastern Anatolia. Rather than take responsibility for the defeat himself, Enver blamed it on the Armenians, who, he claimed, had collaborated with the Russians.

In the aftermath of the battle, the Ottoman Army committed reprisals against the Armenians which quickly developed into what we would now describe as ethnic cleansing. Able-bodied Armenian men were rounded up and massacred, and the women, children, and the elderly were forced to leave the region on foot, often without food and water, in what have become known as "death marches" because so few people survived. The exact scale of the atrocities is not known for certain, but it is now generally accepted that somewhere in the region of 1.5 million Armenians died.

EVIDENCE AND DENIAL

Evidence of what happened in Eastern Anatolia and during the mass deportations comes from eyewitness accounts, reports by journalists, diplomatic communications, and a host of other sources. The American businessman Walter Geddes, for example, was in Aleppo in what is now Syria in September 1915. He recorded the desperate situation of the Armenians he saw there, who had been deported from Eastern Anatolia, describing how hundreds of people were dying every day from starvation. Henry Morgenthau, the American ambassador to the Ottoman Empire, wrote in his memoirs, published in 1919, of receiving reports like those from Geddes on an almost hourly basis. He described what was happening as a "campaign of extermination."

Talaat Pasha, the Ottoman minister of the interior, is now widely held to have been responsible for instigating the policies which led to the massacres. All the official documents relating to the involvement of the Ottoman government were either lost or intentionally destroyed in the chaos following the dissolution of the Ottoman Empire, in what may have been an attempt to hide official responsibility. But some other documentation appears to have survived. In 1919, the Armenian journalist Aram Andonian published a collection of telegrams sent by Talaat to an Ottoman official in Aleppo, which clearly demonstrate that he gave orders for the Armenians to be exterminated. Attempts have been made to cast doubt on the authenticity of the Talaat telegrams as part a wider conspiracy of denial apparently orchestrated by the Turkish government, despite the telegrams being widely accepted as genuine by the vast majority of non-Turkish historians of the period.

— ALTERNATIVE —
THEORIES

One line of argument employed by those who deny that the deaths of 1.5 million Armenians in 1915 constituted genocide is that genocide had not been recognized in international law as being a crime at that time. The word was first used in 1944 by the Polish lawyer Raphael Lemkin, who was of Jewish descent, in reference to the Holocaust, and he was instrumental in the Genocide Convention being adopted by the United Nations in 1948, making it a specific crime. Lemkin cited the Armenian Genocide as being one of the inspirations for his work, making it difficult to argue that the murder of 1.5 million people was not genocide simply because they died before 1944.

Above: The burial of massacred Armenians in a mass grave in Erzurum bears unmistakable similarities to the atrocities carried out during the Holocaust.

A number of Turkish academics and writers have been prosecuted for stating that the deaths of so many Armenians amounted to genocide, being charged with "insulting Turkishness." In truth, the weight of evidence that the Ottoman Empire committed genocide is overwhelming, and the Turkish insistence on denying it has done the international image of the country a great deal more harm than any acknowledgement of the truth could possibly do.

WAS THE NAZI PARTY BEHIND THE REICHSTAG FIRE?

Date: February 27, 1933
Location: Berlin, Germany

The Reichstag fire of February 27, 1933, was blamed on a Dutch man apprehended at the scene, but there is speculation that the Nazi Party started the blaze for its own political gain.

At about 9 o'clock on the evening of February 27, a man walking past the Reichstag, the building housing the German parliament, heard the sound of breaking glass and then saw someone climb into the building through a window. He alerted the police, who arrived on the scene within minutes to discover that a fire had started. The fire department arrived shortly afterward, but by that time the fire had taken hold and, before it could be brought under control, it had gutted the building. A man was found inside the building in possession of material that could be used to start a fire and was arrested. He was twenty-four-year-old Marinus van der Lubbe, from the Netherlands; as it would transpire, he had been involved with the Communist party in that country. Adolf Hitler, then the Chancellor of Germany, arrived at the scene shortly afterward and was described by the British journalist Sefton Delmar, also present, as being in a highly agitated state. He immediately claimed that the fire was the beginning of a Communist plot to take over Germany and began to demand that serious action was taken against members of the German Communist Party.

NAZI POWER GRAB

The Great Depression of the early 1930s had been devastating for the German economy, causing hyperinflation and incredibly high rates of unemployment. This had been reflected in politics with the rise of extreme parties of the left and right, notably the German Communist Party and the Nazi Party. In election after election, no one party could gain enough seats to hold a majority in the Reichstag. The results of the poll held in November 1932 left the Communist Party with 17 percent of the votes and the Nazis with 33 percent, which for the Nazis represented a drop of about 4 percent from the previous vote held in February of that year. As Hitler was the leader of the largest party in the Reichstag, President Paul von Hindenburg had appointed him to the position of chancellor, but he had been able to accomplish little because he lacked a majority in parliament.

A further round of elections was due to take place in early March. As the Nazi vote had declined over the course of 1932, it did not look as if Hitler stood any chance of securing the majority he needed in the Reichstag to enable him to begin implementing the radical program of Nazi policies he proposed. The Reichstag fire occurred a few days before the elections, and the following day Hitler persuaded President Hindenburg to issue an emergency decree suspending many of the civil

Above: Contemporary photograph showing the extent of the fire which gutted the Reichstag building on the night of February 27, 1933.

liberties held by German citizens under the constitution of the Weimar Republic of Germany. Among the measures was the suspension of *habeas corpus*, which prevents unlawful imprisonment. The removal of this writ allowed for detention without trial and, beginning immediately, prominent Communists and other Nazi opponents were rounded up and thrown into jail. The leader of the Communist Party, Ernst Torgler, and three Bulgarian Communists who were in Germany at the time were arrested and charged with being involved in the Reichstag fire along with Van der Lubbe. All were later acquitted, with the exception of Van der Lubbe, who was found guilty and executed after a law was enacted to make arson a capital crime.

Above: A Communist Party of Germany (KPD) propaganda poster from 1932. The slogan translates to "End this System."

In the next elections, held on March 6, the Nazi Party secured 44 percent of the vote. This was enough to form a majority coalition government with another right-wing nationalist party, but still short of the two-thirds majority needed under the Weimar constitution to pass the so-called Enabling Act, or *Ermächtigungsgesetz*, which would give Hitler the ability to rule with absolute power. With all the Communist Party members of the Reichstag unable to take up their seats because they were under arrest, the necessary majority was achieved by means of violence and intimidation: the SA, the paramilitary wing of the Nazi Party, also known as the brownshirts, threatened other Reichstag members into either voting for the act or staying away from parliament during the vote. From that point onward, the Reichstag effectively ceased to be the governing body of Germany, which had been transformed into a one-party state under the dictatorship of Hitler.

A NAZI CONSPIRACY?

The way in which Hitler and the Nazi Party took advantage of the Reichstag fire in order to seize absolute power has inevitably led to speculation that they were responsible for starting it in the first place. The only evidence to support this assertion is circumstantial, based on the premise that the Nazis were the principal beneficiaries of the fire, but also because other plots of a similar nature are known to have occurred. In early September 1939, for instance, German forces staged a number of fake attacks supposedly perpetrated by Polish forces on German positions along the Polish border as a pretext to the invasion of Poland, the event which would lead to the outbreak of the Second World War.

One of the first attempts to establish Nazi culpability for the fire was by German Communists in exile, who in September 1933 staged a mock trial in London to examine the evidence. It is perhaps not surprising that the verdict of this trial was that the Nazis were responsible, but in truth, just as the German court

Right: The trial of the five men accused of the Reichstag fire. Four were acquitted, but Marinus van der Lubbe was found guilty and later sentenced to death.

Above: The broken window through which Marinus van der Lubbe was alleged to have climbed to gain access to the Reichstag.

found no evidence to show a Communist conspiracy was involved, nothing concrete existed to expose a Nazi conspiracy either. In any case, Marinus van der Lubbe had been adamant that he had acted alone, stating on a number of occasions that he had started the fire as an anti-Nazi protest in the hope it would lead to more widespread protests across Germany.

No consensus currently exists among historians as to who started the fire, even if most serious scholars of the Nazis' rise to power accept that the most likely scenario is one in which Van der Lubbe acted alone and Hitler exploited the crisis to achieve his ambition of creating a Nazi state. Shortly after Hindenburg's death, on August 2, 1934, the roles of chancellor and president were combined when the Nazi Party staged a referendum in which 88 percent of Germans agreed to the necessary constitutional change. This result was achieved by a combination of vote-rigging and intimidation, with members of the brownshirts positioned outside polling stations to "encourage" people to vote for the change. After the vote, Hitler adopted the title of Führer, literally "leader," and effectively became the dictator of Germany, with all political power resting in his hands. Whoever was ultimately responsible for starting the Reichstag fire, then, it played a crucial role in transforming what had begun as a fringe political movement in Germany into the dominant force in the country, a sequence of events which would have such catastrophic consequences as the Second World War and the Holocaust.

— ALTERNATIVE —
THEORIES

After the elections held in July 1932, Hermann Goering was appointed as president of the Reichstag. This entitled him to the use of a house adjacent to the Reichstag building and connected to it by means of a tunnel. One of the most common conspiracy theories alleging that the Nazis were responsible for the fire suggests that a team of SA agents entered the building through this tunnel, started the fire, and then escaped back through it, leaving Van der Lubbe behind so that it would be possible to place the blame on the communists. One theory names the senior SA officer Karl Ernst as being in command of the operation, with an SA officer named as Hans Georg Gewehr leading the group who set the fire, though it is not clear what evidence these assertions are based on.

At the Nuremberg trials held in the aftermath of the Second World War, General Franz Halder, a senior officer in the German High Command, stated that at a party to celebrate Hitler's birthday which he attended in 1943, Herman

Above: General Franz Halder, shown here in 1948 giving evidence for the prosecution at the Nuremberg trials of Nazi war criminals.

Goering claimed to have ordered the Reichstag fire. While it is only hearsay, it nevertheless provides some support for the theory of Goering's house being used by the SA in an operation to start the fire. A major problem with this theory is that Van der Lubbe had plenty of opportunity after he was arrested to provide details of any plot for which he had been made the scapegoat, and yet he never did.

DID WALL STREET BANKERS PLAN A COUP D'ÉTAT AGAINST ROOSEVELT?

Date: 1933
Location: USA

In 1933 a retired Marine Corps general claimed he had been approached by men who wanted to depose President Franklin D. Roosevelt. Their aim? To install a fascist regime in his place.

Many Americans are justifiably proud of their democratic traditions of republicanism, which stretch back more than two hundred years. One of these traditions is the peaceful transition of power that occurs when an incumbent president is defeated in an election and replaced by the winner. The resulting political stability has contributed greatly to the freedom and prosperity of the United States, particularly when compared to those countries around the world with little or no democratic tradition. Any attempt to interfere with this process by overthrowing a democratically elected U.S. government would, it may be thought, be considered an important event in American history, but the so-called Business Plot is not widely known and has not been thoroughly investigated by historians. One possible reason for this apparent lack of interest is that few people have believed that anybody really considered staging a coup d'état in the United States, so the Business Plot has been dismissed as fiction. But is there any substance to the claims that a coup against President Roosevelt was planned in 1933 and, if so, who was involved?

SMEDLEY BUTLER

At the time of his retirement in 1931 after thirty-three years of service, Major General Smedley Butler held the highest rank then available in the Marine Corps and was its most decorated soldier. He then became an advocate of a number of veterans' associations and stood unsuccessfully in a Republican primary in Pennsylvania to elect a candidate to stand for the U.S. Senate. So, when he said he had been approached by two men, acting on behalf of a group of wealthy businessmen, who asked him to join a conspiracy to overthrow President Roosevelt and install a fascist dictatorship in the United States, he was taken seriously enough for a special committee of the House of Representatives to investigate the matter.

Above: Major General Smedley Butler claimed he had been asked to lead a coup against President Franklin D. Roosevelt.

The committee began hearing testimony in November 1934 and reported in the following February. Butler told how he had first been approached in July 1933 by two men he named as Gerald MacGuire and William Doyle, and had then met with MacGuire on a number of other occasions over the course of the next year. MacGuire held a junior position with a Wall Street investment bank and claimed to represent a group of senior executives from various banks, together with other wealthy businessmen, several politicians, and a number of high-ranking military officers. He claimed that this group collectively considered that the policies adopted by Roosevelt in the New Deal and in coming off the

Above: Wall Street, New York—did a group of Wall Street bankers really try to replace the president with a fascist regime?

gold standard were taking the United States in the direction of socialism, and they wanted to recruit Butler to lead the military part of a coup to forcibly remove Roosevelt from office. MacGuire claimed that half a million veterans could be called upon to take part and, once Roosevelt had been removed from power, Butler would become the dictator of a fascist regime, presumably with members of the group in the background pulling the strings. According to MacGuire, Butler had been chosen because he was held in high regard by former servicemen because of his work with veterans' associations and prominent support for the Bonus March, a protest staged by First World War veterans demanding the early payment of a bonus they had been promised.

REAL OR HOAX?

Butler provided a list of names he had been given by MacGuire, which were then redacted from the final report because the committee decided that the only evidence against them was hearsay. None of them were called to give evidence and, when a number of names leaked out, the individuals concerned laughed off any suggestion that they had been involved in a plot to depose the president. The names of a number of executives from the investment bank J. P. Morgan appeared in the press, together with Robert Sterling Clark, the heir to the Singer Sewing Machine fortune, and Grayson Murphy, who ran the bank for which MacGuire worked, but most newspaper reports treated the alleged plot as a giant hoax.

— ALTERNATIVE —
THEORIES

One name redacted from the final report of the House of Representatives committee was Prescott Bush, the father of President George H. W. Bush and grandfather of President George W. Bush. In the early 1930s, he was a partner in the private bank Brown Brothers Harriman and would later become a U.S. Senator, the first of the Bush family to hold an elected office. Nothing other than hearsay links him to the plot, but it is nevertheless intriguing to imagine that he could have been involved in an attempt to abolish the office his son and grandson would both go on to hold.

Above: Prescott Bush, the Wall Street banker who became the first member of the Bush dynasty to hold an elected office in the United States.

Despite the committee's apparent unwillingness to confront any of the figures alleged to have been involved in the plot, it did give some credence to what Butler had told them. Now, more than eighty years later, there remains no reason to doubt Butler, who had a spotless reputation and did not stand to gain anything by revealing the plot. In the 1930s, there were certainly fascist sympathizers among the wealthy elite of the United States. But it is impossible to know if the plot described by Butler was a genuine attempt to organize a coup d'état, or if it amounted to nothing more than idle talk between men who thought their wealth gave them the right to dictate how the United States government should be run.

IS THE BILDERBERG GROUP REALLY A SECRET WORLD GOVERNMENT?

Date: 1954 onwards
Location: Europe and USA

Conspiracy theorists have alleged that, since its inception, the real purpose of the secretive Bilderberg Group has been to lay the groundwork for a single world government.

The first conference took place over the course of a weekend in 1954 at the Bilderberg Hotel in the small town of Oosterbeek, near Arnhem in the Netherlands, and was made up of about sixty delegates drawn from the ruling elites of the United States and Western European countries. Its stated purpose was to provide a forum for discussions aimed at promoting cooperation and understanding between countries with advanced industrial economies in the West. At the first meeting, subjects on the agenda included European integration, attitudes toward the Soviet Union, and economic policies and problems. Participants included both current and former senior politicians and diplomats, military leaders, industrialists and financiers, media executives, academics, and a range of others who were prominent in their fields. The perceived success of the first meeting led to the conference becoming an annual event, held over a single weekend at a European or American venue, and with the agenda set and delegates invited by a steering committee. Today the number of delegates has increased to about 150 and the agenda broadened to take in whatever subjects the steering committee decides are relevant, though usually still drawn from the fields of international relations and economics. Otherwise, the meetings are held along the same lines as that first one.

Above: The Bilderberg Hotel in Oosterbeek, which gave its name to the Bilderberg Group, was the venue for its first meeting.

TALKING SHOP OR WORLD GOVERNMENT?

This may all sound innocuous enough: a talking shop for people who enjoy the sound of their own voices. But what has set the Bilderberg Group apart from the usual run of international conferences, and has excited conspiracy theorists, are the people who have attended meetings and the fact that all discussions are held in private. Over the years, participants have included U.S. presidents, including George H. W. Bush and Bill Clinton; British prime ministers Margaret Thatcher and Tony Blair; German Chancellor Angela Merkel; and such prominent businesspeople as Bill Gates of Microsoft and Jeff Bezos of Amazon.

The reason for the secrecy is, according to the organizers, to allow people whose every word usually comes under intense scrutiny to speak freely without having to worry that what they say will be taken out of context and splashed across the world's media. But it also creates a situation in which the global power elite rub shoulders with each other while the rest of us have no idea what

Above: Hilary Clinton was at the 1997 Bilderberg conference, six years after her husband had attended.

they are talking about. This provides a space that conspiracy theorists can fill with whatever ideas take their fancy, in the knowledge that no details of the actual proceedings will emerge to contradict them. Most of the resulting theories have clearly been put forward by people with their own axes to grind. Right-wing extremists, for instance, think the Bilderberg Group has been laying the foundations for the imposition of a global planned economy in the style of the former Soviet Union. Meanwhile, those on the left regard it more as an attempt by transnational corporations and such financial institutions as J. P. Morgan and Goldman Sachs to direct the process of globalization to their own advantage.

KINGMAKERS

Another strand of conspiracy theory does not impose quite such grand schemes on the Bilderberg Group, rather seeing it as an insidious means by which its members can exert their influence on global politics. One way they achieve this, according to the theory at least, is by inviting up-and-coming politicians to attend and, if they meet requirements, supporting them financially and through the media in their subsequent rise to the top. Conspiracy theorists point to the examples of Bill Clinton, who attended in 1991 when he was the Governor of Arkansas and was elected as U.S. President the following year, and Tony Blair, who was invited to the meeting in 1993, became leader of the Labour Party in 1994 and the British prime minister three years later.

The obvious problem with this theory is that numerous political leaders from around the world have never had anything to do with the Bilderberg Group, while many politicians who have attended have not gone on to achieve high office. Hillary Clinton was at the

— ALTERNATIVE —
THEORIES

Conspiracy theories about the Bilderberg Group being a secret world government have deflected attention away from a genuine concern associated with the secret nature of the meetings. Wealthy industrialists and financiers are provided with privileged access in off-the-record surroundings to elected politicians who may be involved in enacting and administering the regulations governing their business activities. Once contacts have been established, the potential exists for favors to be exchanged, which may not be in the best interests of the wider public. This is a polite way of suggesting that the secrecy could act as

Above: Ben Bernanke, then Chairman of the Federal Reserve, leaving the 2008 Bilderberg Conference. We can only guess at what is discussed at such meetings.

a shield for such corrupt practices as retired politicians being given lucrative directorships of companies that have prospered during their period in office.

meeting in 1997, but Donald Trump, as far as we know, has never been invited to attend and, in his anti-globalization "America first" rhetoric, has frequently expressed opinions diametrically opposed to the founding principles of the group. This could suggest that the Bilderberg Group are not quite the influential kingmakers they would like to be. Perhaps the reality is rather more mundane, and the group is in fact little more than a back-slapping exercise between people who like to think of themselves as belonging to the global elite when the true picture may be somewhat different.

WHAT WAS THE PURPOSE OF THE WATERGATE BURGLARY?

Date: June 17, 1972
Location: Washington, D.C., USA

The arrest of five men who had broken into the Watergate Complex in Washington led to President Nixon's resignation, but the reason for the burglary remains clouded in suspicion.

Shortly after midnight on June 17, 1972, a security guard at the Watergate Office Building, part of the Watergate Complex in the Foggy Bottom district of Washington, D.C., noticed duct tape on the latches of doors leading to the offices of the Democratic National Committee (DNC), the governing body of the Democratic Party. He removed the tape, which was preventing the doors from locking shut, but an hour later found that it had been replaced, prompting him to call the police. The five men found in the offices and arrested by the police had been engaged in wiretapping telephones and photographing documents. They had contact details on them for G. Gordon Liddy and E. Howard Hunt. Both were members of the so-called White House Plumbers, a unit originally set up within the White House to prevent information that could be damaging to President Nixon from leaking out. Under the direction of the Committee for the Re-election of the President (CRP), the unit had apparently branched out into gathering information on the Democratic Party using a variety of methods, some of which, such as breaking and entering, were obviously illegal.

THE SMOKING GUN

Over the course of the following two years, investigations gradually brought the scandal closer and closer to Nixon. The journalists Bob Woodward and Carl Bernstein wrote a series of articles in the *Washington Post* based on information they had been given by an informant named as Deep Throat, later revealed to be Mark Felt, the deputy director of the FBI. His advice to them had been to "follow the money," and this led to the revelation that the CRP had been using a slush fund to run a dirty tricks campaign against the Democrats, forcing Nixon to sack a number of its members. One of these was John Dean, who gave evidence to a Senate Select Committee that Nixon had been secretly recording all of the meetings that had taken place in the Oval Office of the White House.

Above: Demonstrators approaching the Capitol Building in Washington in October 1973 to demand that Congress impeach President Nixon.

A lengthy legal battle ensued, which resulted in Nixon being compelled by a Supreme Court subpoena to hand over the tapes he had made. Nothing on the tapes implicated Nixon in ordering the Watergate burglary, or even knowing about it before it had taken place, but there was nevertheless enough evidence to show that he had been involved in the subsequent cover-up and had been well aware of some of the CRP's other illegal activities. The final straw for Nixon came on August 5, 1974, with the release of what became known as the "smoking gun" tape, a recording made of a meeting held six days after the burglary in which Nixon discussed the possibility of using the CIA to obstruct the ongoing FBI investigation. Congressional impeachment proceedings had already begun against the president and any remaining support he had among senators and congressmen now evaporated. On August 8, and with the threat of imminent impeachment hanging over him, Nixon resigned the presidency, but was not subsequently charged with committing any offense after being granted a pardon by his successor, President Gerald Ford.

THE HOWARD HUGHES CONNECTION

It would later emerge that the DNC offices in the Watergate Complex had been broken into a few weeks before the burglary in which the five men were arrested. During this first break-in, two telephones had been tapped, but one of the taps had not worked properly, leading to speculation that the primary objective of the second break-in was to replace the broken tap. While this remains a possibility, installing a new tap would have taken a

Left: E. Howard Hunt, one of the White House Plumbers, was convicted of involvement in the Watergate burglary and served thirty-three months in prison.

Right: Nixon in April 1974 preparing to address the nation about the release of edited transcripts of the Oval Office recordings.

matter of minutes and the burglars spent more than two hours in the DNC offices, suggesting that there must have been a further purpose to the break-in. None of the burglars or Liddy or Hunt, who admitted their involvement, provided full explanations of their motives, leading to the development of a number of theories concerning their intentions.

The burglars could simply have been looking for any dirt they could find on the Democrats which could be used against them in the upcoming presidential elections scheduled for November of that year; but they could also have been looking for something specific. One theory alleges that the underlying motive for the burglary was the convoluted relationship which had developed between Nixon and the reclusive oil tycoon Howard Hughes, which certainly gives the impression of involving corruption.

In 1957, Hughes had loaned $200,000 to Nixon's brother Donald, ostensibly to bail out a failing business venture, but the loan had never been repaid. Details of the loan had come out during the 1960 presidential election campaign, fought between Nixon and John F. Kennedy, and the publicity surrounding it could well have

Above: A filing cabinet from the Democratic National Committee's office that was broken into during the burglary.

contributed to Nixon's narrow defeat. In the run-up to the 1968 election, which was won by Nixon, Hughes is thought to have channeled large sums of money to Nixon through his friend and business associate Charles "Bebo" Rebozo. Once he had been elected, Nixon is alleged to have done a number of favors for Hughes in return.

The chairman of the DNC at the time of the break-in was Larry O'Brien, who had previously worked for Hughes as a political lobbyist, potentially giving him access to knowledge of the payments Hughes had made to Nixon through Rebozo. O'Brien's office was in the Watergate Complex, leading to speculation that the burglars were trying to find out if he really had any dirt on Nixon or that they were looking for anything which could be used against O'Brien to keep him quiet. When later asked if he was in possession of any incriminating evidence concerning Nixon and Hughes, O'Brien said that, had he been, there would have been no need for anybody to break into his office to get it, because it would have been all over the front pages of the newspapers.

Nixon always maintained his innocence over the Watergate scandal, famously saying in a television address to the nation a few months before he resigned that he was not a crook. Even if he had not known about the break-in beforehand, however, he was clearly involved in the subsequent cover-up and attempts to obstruct the investigation into it, which was more than enough to make him unfit to be president. We may never know the purpose of the Watergate break-in for certain, but it proved to be one dirty trick too far for Richard Nixon.

— ALTERNATIVE —
THEORIES

Neither of the wire taps put in place by the Watergate burglars was on Larry O'Brien's telephone, suggesting that he may not have been the primary target. Rumors have long circulated that the real purpose of the Watergate break-in was to gather information on the involvement of people who worked for the DNC in a prostitution ring which is known to have operated out of a block of apartments neighboring the Watergate Complex. It had been alleged these people were arranging dates with the call girls in the apartment block on behalf of well-known figures in the Democratic Party, which, had it come to light, would have been extremely damaging.

The man who had been hired to monitor the wiretaps, named as former FBI agent Alfred Baldwin, testified to a congressional investigation that he had kept written logs of the telephone conversations he had listened to on the bugged lines, but did not record them. It is not clear what happened to these logs after the break-in was discovered,

Above: The Watergate Hotel and Office Building, part of the complex where the burglary took place. The DNC offices were on the sixth floor.

and no details or names of anybody who may have been involved have since emerged. In the absence of any corroborating evidence, it is currently impossible to say for certain if there is any substance to these allegations, but it does suggest that shady dealings within U.S. political parties at the time of the Watergate scandal may not have been the sole preserve of Richard Nixon and the Republicans.

ESPIONAGE AND COVERT OPERATIONS

The job of secret agents is to carry out covert operations and, where they have been successful, the rest of us are unlikely to be any the wiser. In this section, we deal with instances where the clandestine activities of spies have either been exposed to some extent or are at least suspected, even if it has not always been possible to tell for certain exactly who has done what.

We look at the possible involvement of the British intelligence services in forging the so-called Black Diaries of Sir Roger Casement and the reason why Rudolf Hess flew to Britain during the Second World War. We also consider whether Russian agents were responsible for forging the *Protocols of the Elders of Zion*, an anti-Semitic tract supposedly detailing Jewish plans for world domination, and if German saboteurs caused the massive explosion at Black Tom Island in New York Harbor during the First World War. We then explore rumors of a British prime minister being a Soviet agent and discuss why the British government protected the identity of a man known to have been a spy, before bringing the book up to recent times by discussing what the Pakistani intelligence service knew of the whereabouts of Osama bin Laden. After delving into this murky world of spies and surveillance, we may not come up with all the answers, but we can at least attempt to expose some of the lies and deceit on which the world of espionage is based.

Left: Harold Wilson, the British prime minister alleged to have been a Soviet agent.

WHO WROTE THE PROTOCOLS OF THE ELDERS OF ZION?

Date: 1903
Location: Russia and France

The *Protocols of the Elders of Zion* has been exposed as a crude forgery aimed at stirring up anti-Semitism, but the author of this hateful text remains a mystery.

The text was first published in 1903 in serial form in a Russian newspaper and later collected together as part of a book, before being translated into a number of other European languages and widely distributed across the continent and in the United States. It was supposedly taken from the proceedings of the First Zionist Congress, a conference held in Basel, Switzerland, in 1897. This gathering had been arranged by Theodor Herzl, sometimes known as the father of Zionism, was where the goal of establishing a Jewish homeland in Palestine was set out. The *Protocols of the Elders of Zion* does not mention Zionism at all, consisting instead of twenty-four chapters which purport to outline the methods a Jewish conspiracy would use to achieve world domination. A cabal of Jewish bankers, for instance, was said to be working together to dominate the world's

Right: The First Zionist Congress. The *Protocols of the Elders of Zion* were alleged to have been taken from the proceedings of the congress.

financial markets, while another plot was supposedly engaged in efforts to take control of the world's major media outlets.

SPREADING ANTI-SEMITISM

The *Protocols* appeared in Russia at a time when a wave of anti-Jewish pogroms was occurring across the country, and may have been an attempt either to incite further attacks or to justify the violence in which, it has been estimated, at least two thousand Jews were killed. As the book was translated and disseminated, it was also used to justify anti-Semitism in other parts of Europe and in the United States. It was cited by Adolf Hitler in *Mein Kampf*, the book setting out his political ideology, which he wrote in 1924 while serving a prison sentence for the Munich Beer Hall Putsch he had led in the previous year. Hitler may have first become aware of the *Protocols* through a German edition of *The International Jew*. This was a collection of anti-Semitic articles from the *Dearborn Independent*, the newspaper owned by the pioneering car manufacturer Henry Ford. In 1920, Ford had sponsored an American edition of the *Protocols*, and he would continue to claim that it was evidence of a Jewish conspiracy to take over the world long after it had been thoroughly debunked.

In 1921, *The Times* newspaper in London ran a series of articles by Philip Graves, its foreign correspondent in Istanbul, which conclusively showed that large tracts of the *Protocols* had been plagiarized from a novel published in 1864 by the French writer Maurice Joly, entitled *The Dialogue in Hell Between Machiavelli and Montesquieu*. Further investigations by others found more examples of plagiarism from other sources, including from the writings of Theodor Herzl, which altogether comprehensively destroyed claims that the *Protocols* were an authentic record of the proceedings of the First Zionist Congress. Henry Ford would later accept that it was a forgery and apologize for his role in disseminating the book in the United States, but many other anti-Semites have continued to cite it as a legitimate source for their accusations of a Jewish conspiracy to take over the world.

AUTHORSHIP

Once the *Protocols* had been exposed as a forgery, attempts were made to discover the identity of the author. Copies are thought to have been in circulation in Paris before it first appeared in Russia, leading to the suggestion that it was written in the French capital. The most likely source appears to have been Matvei Golovinski, a Russian journalist and writer then living in Paris. Golovinski is thought to have been an agent for Okhrana, the secret service of Imperial Russia. He is known to have written propaganda pamphlets for Pyotr Rachkovsky, the head of the Okhrana office in Paris, and to have worked on the same French newspaper as Charles Joly, the son of the author of the novel on which much of the *Protocols* was based. Comparisons between the writing style of Golovinski's known work and the *Protocols* have indicated that he may have been its author, but, in truth, neither this nor the circumstantial evidence used to identify him provide definitive proof, instead only suggesting that he is the most likely candidate.

The identity of the author, then, remains in doubt, but that does not alter the fact of the *Protocols* being a forgery produced by

— ALTERNATIVE —
THEORIES

At a trial held in 1935 in Berne, Switzerland, in which the Swiss distributors of the *Protocols* were prosecuted under the country's obscenity laws, Ulrich Fleischhauer, an expert witness for the defense, claimed that the text was genuine and really had been presented at the First Zionist Congress. He argued that it had been written by the well-known Jewish intellectual and author Ahad Ha'am, but could provide no evidence for this assertion. The prosecution produced an overwhelming body of evidence, including a written deposition by Philip Graves, which convinced the court that the *Protocols* were forgeries.

Above: The author Ahad Ha'am—allegations made at the Berne trial that he had written the *Protocols* were shown to be totally without foundation.

anti-Semites with the intention of stirring up further hatred against Jews. The theory of a Jewish conspiracy to take over the world did not begin with the *Protocols*, but the widespread acceptance of the text as genuine in the early half of the twentieth century and beyond certainly contributed to a rising tide of anti-Semitism. Despite being exposed as a forgery more than ninety years ago, it is still cited by anti-Semitic conspiracy theorists today, presumably because they have little else on which to base their poisonous views.

WERE THE BLACK DIARIES OF SIR ROGER CASEMENT FORGERIES?

Date: 1916
Location: UK

For more than a hundred years it has been debated whether the Black Diaries of Sir Roger Casement are real or if they were forged by the British secret services as a means to discredit a martyr.

R oger Casement was arrested on April 21, 1916, after coming ashore on the west coast of Ireland from a German U-boat. He had traveled to Ireland from Germany, where he had been soliciting support from the German government for the republican rebels in Ireland, who were planning a rising against British rule. A German ship carrying arms for the rebels was following Casement, but was intercepted by the Royal Navy before the rising began on Easter Monday, three days after Casement's arrest. He was charged with treason and transferred to a prison in London to await trial. Before the trial began on June 26, excerpts from five diaries that it was claimed had been found among his possessions began to leak out in the press. The Black Diaries, as they were later named, contained graphic details of homosexual encounters between

Casement and young men, some of whom he had paid for their services. It appeared to be a calculated effort by the British establishment to discredit him ahead of the expected guilty verdict, in an attempt to sway public opinion against him and reduce calls for clemency in the likely event of the death sentence being imposed.

THE IRISH REPUBLICAN

Casement was born in Dublin to a Protestant Anglo-Irish family and had converted to Catholicism at an early age. He became well known as a consequence of two reports he had written as a consul for the British Foreign Office concerning the human rights abuses he had witnessed against the indigenous people of the Belgian Congo and Peru, work for which he received a knighthood. His experiences of the abuse of power by colonial administrations overseas appear to have motivated him to become more fully involved in the Irish republican movement and, in 1913, he retired from the Foreign Office to devote himself to the cause. The issue of home rule for Ireland had been debated in Britain for decades by that time, complicated by the Unionists in the north of Ireland, who were demanding that Ireland remain in the United Kingdom. Most of the republican groups in the south of the country had suspended their activities at the outbreak of the First World War, but a small number considered that the war presented them with an opportunity to push for independence while the rest of Britain was focused on fighting against Germany.

Above: Roger Casement. In 1911 he was knighted for his humanitarian work in the Congo and Peru, but in 1916 was executed for treason.

In October 1914, Casement traveled to Germany as an unofficial ambassador for the Irish republican movement in the hope of gaining support for Irish independence from the German government. His mission was only partially successful in that the

Left: A painting of the Easter Rising by Walter Paget. Casement was arrested while attempting to bring German arms to the rebels.

German government agreed to issue a declaration in support of an independent Ireland, but did not agree to his request to send a force of German soldiers to help the republican rising against British rule. As well as negotiating with the Germans, Casement attempted to recruit a brigade of volunteers from among the Irish soldiers being held as prisoners of war in Germany, who could be sent to Ireland to fight in the event of a rising. He could only persuade about fifty men to agree to join, no doubt because by doing so they would have been committing treason.

Casement appears to have traveled back to Ireland in April 1916 with the intention of persuading the republican leadership to postpone the rising because he had not secured as much German support as he had hoped. After his arrest, the Easter Rising went ahead as planned, beginning in Dublin on Easter Monday and lasting for five days before being put down with overwhelming force. The heavy-handed response of the British included executing fourteen of the rising's leadership after they had been court-martialed in secret. This, perhaps as much as the rising itself, caused a huge increase in support, in Ireland and beyond, for the republican cause of establishing an independent Ireland.

A FORGED LIFE?

Casement was the last of the men involved in the rising to face trial, and the release of excerpts of his diaries can be regarded as a reaction to the widespread public outrage at the treatment of the men who had already been executed. At that time, homosexuality was illegal in Britain and was the subject of particular disapproval among the Catholic community in Ireland, from which the majority of Irish republicans were drawn. As well as being an attempt to discredit Casement, the British authorities may also have been trying to distract attention away from the situation in Ireland by focusing instead on a man who had undoubtedly committed treason by consorting with the enemy at a time of war. After the contents of the diaries were made public, Casement's family and friends disputed the accusations that he was homosexual, though, as it was illegal, it was not unusual at that time for homosexual men to lead double lives in which their true sexuality remained hidden.

Accusations that the British secret services, specifically MI5, had forged the diaries began shortly after the first entries had been leaked and have continued ever since, particularly among those

Right: An illustration from May 1916 of Roger Casement on trial for treason in London. He was found guilty and sentenced to death.

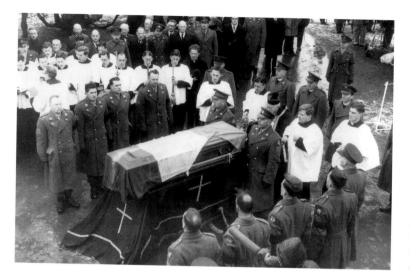

Left: In 1965 Casement's remains were transferred from London to Dublin, where he was given a state funeral as a hero of the Irish Republic.

members of the Irish republican community who regard Casement as a hero of the struggle for independence and a martyr to the cause. The full diaries were not declassified until 1959, when they became available for public inspection. A forensic examination conducted in 2002 came to the conclusion that the diaries were real, largely based on a comparison of the handwriting with known examples of Casement's other writings, but these findings have since been disputed.

Opinion remains divided today, but, in the end, there can be little doubt that the British government used the diaries, whether they were real or fake, as a means of ensuring that Casement would face the death penalty and so that his execution would not lead to a further increase in support for the republican cause. As attitudes to homosexuality have slowly changed in Ireland since his death, Casement has come to be seen not only as a hero of the Irish independence movement, but as a symbol of the struggle to achieve equal rights for all members of Irish society, whatever their religion or sexuality.

— ALTERNATIVE —
THEORIES

In 1999, a secret memo written by an MI5 operative named Frank Hall, four days before Casement was hanged, was found at the Public Records Office in Kew. The memo shed some light on one of the men alluded to in the diaries. A number of entries in the diary from 1911 describe Casement going to Belfast to meet a man named only as Millar, stating that the two were involved in a homosexual relationship. Hall appears to have gone to Belfast after the diaries were discovered to look for the man named as Millar, whose existence would provide corroborating evidence that the diaries were real.

Above: Roger Casement c. 1904—disagreements about the Black Diaries continue, but the available evidence points to them being real.

Hall found a man he named as Joseph Millar Gordon, who worked as a bank clerk in Belfast and could be connected to Casement through a motorcycle Casement had bought for him. This does not prove that Casement was in a homosexual relationship with Joseph Millar, but it does indicate that the diaries were likely real, because at least one of the men mentioned by name existed and the two had known each other. If the diaries were fake, whoever forged them must have known about the relationship between Casement and Millar, which, while not impossible, is not very likely either. Since the emergence of the memo, it has been claimed that it was produced as part of the smear campaign against Casement; but, if that was the case, then the details it contained would surely have been released to the press at the time rather than kept secret.

WHO WAS BEHIND THE BLACK TOM EXPLOSION?

Date: July 30, 1916
Location: New York Harbor, USA

The huge explosion at Black Tom Island in New York Harbor was initially thought to have been an accident, but could German secret agents have been involved?

At the time of the explosion in July 1916, Black Tom Island was connected to the New Jersey side of the harbor by a causeway, and was being used as a depot for storing American-made munitions and explosives due to be shipped to Europe. The United States had not yet entered the First World War and remained officially neutral, allowing the sale of war materials to both sides. In practice, the Royal Navy blockade of German ports, imposed in the first days of the war in August 1914, had proved so effective that no merchant ship could get through, restricting trade from the United States to Britain and France. The German response had been to begin a campaign of unrestricted submarine warfare in the North Atlantic, in an effort to stop American war materials and supplies from reaching the Allies. As we have seen in a previous chapter, the sinking of the *Lusitania* by a German U-boat in May 1915 (see page 70) caused a major diplomatic incident between the United States and Germany

Right: Black Tom Island shortly after the explosion. The wreckage of the warehouses gives an indication of the scale of the blast.

and, though this stopped short of the United States declaring war, Germany suspended its U-boat campaign. From then onward, the Germans decided to concentrate their efforts on covert ways of disrupting the trade by encouraging strikes among American workers, and using secret agents to carry out acts of sabotage against factories and transport systems.

THE EXPLOSION

On the night of July 30, 1916, more than 50 tons of TNT, together with large quantities of other explosives and munitions, were being stored on Black Tom Island in warehouses, freight cars, and barges moored along its piers. Shortly after midnight, a number of small fires began around the depot, which were initially thought to have spread from smudge pots lit by security guards to deter mosquitoes. Efforts to stop the fires spreading failed and, at about 2 a.m., an enormous explosion occurred. This was followed by a number of smaller blasts which destroyed the depot and are thought to have killed between five and ten people. The first explosion broke windows in Jersey City and Manhattan, and debris from the blast damaged the Statue of Liberty across the harbor. Access to Lady Liberty's lamp, gained through a narrow

Above: Franz von Rintelen, the German agent known to have committed acts of sabotage and suspected of involvement in the Black Tom explosion.

passage inside the statue's arm, had to be stopped for reasons of public safety, and the passageway remains closed to the public today.

GERMAN SABOTEURS

The police investigation into the explosions quickly established that the fires had been started deliberately. Suspicion fell on German saboteurs, who were thought to have been behind a number of unexplained factory fires in the months leading up to the explosion. In 1915, the British had caught a German secret agent in London going under the name of Horst von der Goltz who, with the threat of execution hanging over him, had admitted to being involved in a number of acts of sabotage in the United States. The British sent him to the States to stand trial and, on the Atlantic crossing, his police escort allowed him to talk to an American journalist. Reports of his activities soon appeared in newspapers, and rumors circulated of German dynamiters being on the loose in the United States. This increased the anti-German feeling that had been aroused by the sinking of the *Lusitania* (see page 70) and led many Americans to assume that German agents were responsible for the incident on Black Tom Island.

The police failed to find a connection to any German plot and it would be decades before details began to emerge. In the 1930s, insurance investigators found links to the German government through Johann Heinrich von Bernstorff, the German ambassador to the United States from 1914 to 1917, and a naval attaché called Franz von Rintelen. In reality, Rintelen was an intelligence officer who is now known to have used so-called pencil bombs, small incendiary devices with timer fuses. It's now thought that similar bombs could have been used to start the fires on Black Tom Island, and a number of known German agents have been implicated in the

— ALTERNATIVE —
THEORIES

Irish-American republican groups such as the Irish Republican Brotherhood and Clan na Gael may have played a role in the Black Tom explosion, though the leadership of both organizations denied having anything to do with it. Links between the groups and Johann Heinrich von Bernstorff certainly existed and, with Germany agreeing to help the cause of Irish independence in 1916, a reciprocal arrangement could have been in place. Irish workers in American ports are thought to have helped Franz von Rintelen to plant pencil bombs in the holds of merchant ships, so it would not be a great leap to suggest that they also helped German agents gain access to the Black Tom munitions depot.

Above: Johann Heinrich von Bernstorff, the German ambassador to the United States who forged links with Irish republicans in New York.

plot; these included Kurt Jahnke and Lothar Witzke, both of whom were in the United States at the time, though no direct evidence has conclusively linked them to the fires. In 1935 an insurance claim for $50 million was made to the Nazi regime then in power in Germany. The government refused to pay, but after the Second World War the claim was settled, the final payment being made in 1979, indicating that German agents must have been responsible, even if the exact details remain unknown.

DID NAZI SECRET AGENTS PLAN TO KIDNAP THE DUKE OF WINDSOR?

Date: 1940
Location: Lisbon, Portugal

A Nazi plot to kidnap one man may appear quite inconsequential, but when that man is the Duke of Windsor, the scheme takes on an altogether deeper significance.

The Duke of Windsor, the former King Edward VIII, abdicated the British throne in December 1936 to marry the American divorcee Wallis Simpson. The marriage caused a rift to open up between Edward and his younger brother, who became King George VI, not least because of Edward's belief that Wallis, the Duchess of Windsor, had been slighted by a British refusal to grant her the title of Her Royal Highness after they were married. Rumors persisted that Edward's desire to marry Wallis had not been the real reason for the abdication and that he had been forced out by the British government because of his attempts to increase the power of the monarchy and because there may have been some truth to allegations that both he and the duchess were Nazi sympathizers. In October 1937, the couple visited Germany and met Adolf Hitler and other leading Nazis, adding fuel to

Right: Suspicions about the loyalties of the Duke and Duchess of Windsor grew when, in 1937, they met with Adolf Hitler in Germany.

the speculation about where their loyalties lay. They became the subject of a number of conspiracy theories, principally that, had Germany invaded Britain during the Second World War, the duke would have been restored to the throne to become a puppet leader of a British Nazi state.

LISBON

In September 1939 the duke was given the rank of major general in the British Army and the job of liaising with the British and French armies assembled in northern France to repel the expected German invasion. In early May the following year, the invasion began and, with lightning speed, the German army broke through the British and French defenses. France fell in six weeks and the duke and duchess, who were still in the country at the time, escaped across the border into neutral Spain. At the beginning of July 1940, British concerns about the friendly relationship between the Spanish government and Nazi Germany led to the couple moving on to Portugal, where they settled in a villa on the coast near Estoril, about 20 miles from Lisbon. Portugal was also neutral, but its long-standing ties with Britain meant that it

Above: The Duke and Duchess of Windsor at the villa near Estoril where they stayed in July 1940 before leaving Portugal for the Bahamas.

was considered a safer place for the duke and duchess to live while the British government decided what to do with them.

Lisbon was at the center of all sorts of covert operations, and numerous secret agents from both sides operated in the city throughout the war, often rubbing shoulders with each other at the casino in Estoril. At the same time, both Britain and Germany attempted to gain favor with the government of Antonio Salazar, because Portugal supplied both sides with tungsten, a vital component in the manufacture of the hardened steel used in armor plating and artillery shells. The arrival of the duke and duchess complicated matters even further, and the British government wanted them to return to British soil as soon as possible to get them away from the influence of Nazi agents.

OPERATION WILLI

King George VI refused to allow the duke and duchess to return to Britain so, shortly after they arrived in Portugal, the duke was offered the governorship of the Bahamas, which at that time was a British overseas territory. Edward was apparently unimpressed with the offer, but, as he was still an officer in the British Army, Winston Churchill threatened him with a court martial if he refused it. Even so, the couple lingered in Portugal for the whole of July, and it would later emerge that during this period they were contacted a number of times by people acting on behalf of Nazi Germany.

The details of exactly what happened are not known in full, but a cache of German diplomatic telegrams published in 1957 has shed some light on an apparent conspiracy between Germany and Spain, in which senior members of the Spanish government attempted to entice the duke and duchess to return to Spain from Portugal. They were visited at their villa in Estoril at least twice by emissaries from the Spanish government, who invited them to come to Spain on a hunting trip. They were offered the use of a large house and sufficient funds for them to live in the style to which they were accustomed; while it appears that, unknown to them, Germany was planning to prevent them from leaving Spain, by force if required, so that the duke would be readily accessible in the event of an invasion of Britain.

While the duke and duchess were still in Portugal, perhaps attempting to make up their minds between going to the Bahamas or back to Spain, Walter Schellenberg, one of Germany's top intelligence agents, arrived in Lisbon with the apparent intention of assessing the viability of Operation Willi. This was the code name given to a plan to kidnap the duke in Portugal if he did not willingly agree to return to Spain. The extent to which this plan was actually put into operation remains unknown, and Schellenberg would write after the war that he had not believed it to be feasible. In the event, the operation did not go ahead, perhaps because of fears it would have led to a major diplomatic incident between Germany and Portugal, which would have put the continued supply of tungsten at risk.

On August 1, 1940, the duke and duchess finally set sail for the Bahamas, where they would remain out of the reach of German agents for the duration of the war. On the same day, Hitler ordered the German Luftwaffe to gain air superiority over the

Above: Walter Schellenberg, one of Germany's top intelligence agents, was sent to Portugal in July 1941 to assess the feasability of the plot to kidnap the duke.

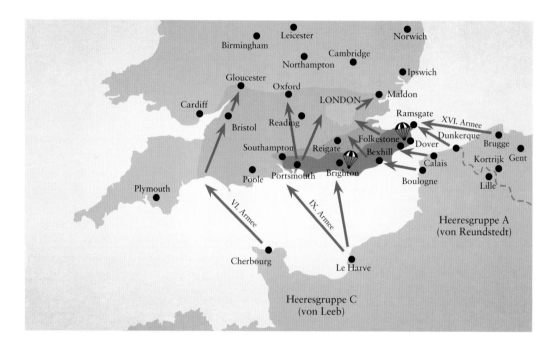

Leicester
Birmingham
Norwich
Cambridge
Northampton
Gloucester
Ipswich
Oxford
Cardiff
LONDON
Maldon
Bristol
Reading
Ramsgate
XVI. Armee
Southampton
Reigate
Folkestone
Dover
Dunkerque
Brugge
Bexhill
Kortrijk   Gent
Poole   Portsmouth   Brighton
Calais
Plymouth
Boulogne
Lille
VI. Armee
IX. Armee
Heeresgruppe A
(von Reundstedt)
Cherbourg
Le Harve
Heeresgruppe C
(von Leeb)

Above: Operation Sea Lion, the German plan to invade Britain in 1940 and, perhaps, to install the Duke of Windsor as a Nazi leader of Britain.

RAF, the main objective of the Battle of Britain and the essential first step in Operation Sea Lion, the German plan for the invasion of the United Kingdom. Some military historians think that Hitler did not actually intend to invade Britain, instead using the threat of invasion as a means of drawing the British to the negotiating table. If this was the case, then the intrigues surrounding the duke and duchess could have been part of this overall strategy, making the British think that the duke was the target of a kidnapping plot so that he could be installed as the leader of Britain after an invasion, when the Germans had little or no intention of carrying out any such operation. The duke's loyalty to Britain appears to have been tested by German advances, but in the end, whether by force or by free choice, he chose not to become a traitor.

— ALTERNATIVE —
THEORIES

In his role as a liaison officer in northern France, the Duke of Windsor toured the positions of the French army along the border with Germany and Belgium. Unknown to the French, he wrote a number of reports for British intelligence concerning what he considered to be the unprepared state of the French army. He also identified a number of weak points in the line, including around the town of Sedan. When the German offensive began in May 1940, it involved a blitzkrieg attack through the Ardennes forest in Belgium, to invade France through the weak point at Sedan. Allegations surfaced after the war that the reports written by the duke, which were largely ignored by the British, had been passed to the Germans by either the duke or the duchess.

It is rumored that in 1937 the duchess had an affair with Joachim von Ribbentrop, who was at that time the German ambassador to Britain and would later become the foreign minister in Hitler's government. Conspiracy theorists

Above: The Duchess of Windsor in the Bahamas in late 1940. The FBI considered that both she and her husband represented a security risk.

suggest that, as well as having an affair, the Duchess passed secret intelligence obtained from her husband to Von Ribbentrop. An FBI investigation into the conduct of the duke and duchess while they were in the Bahamas reached the conclusion that she represented a security risk, but it is not known for certain if she really did pass secret intelligence to the Germans during the war.

WHY DID RUDOLF HESS FLY TO BRITAIN?

Date: May 1941
Location: Scotland, UK

The Rudolf Hess affair was one of the most bizarre episodes of the Second World War. Now, more than seventy years later, it remains far from clear what was really going on.

At about 11 o'clock on the night of May 10, 1941, Rudolf Hess, the deputy führer of Germany and close friend of Adolf Hitler, parachuted out of the Messerschmitt Bf 110 he was piloting over Scotland and landed to the south of Glasgow. He was found by a local farmer who helped him to his cottage nearby before handing him over to the Home Guard. Later that night, Hess was taken to a police station where he was questioned. He claimed to be Captain Alfred Horn and said he was carrying a message for the Duke of Hamilton, a leading member of the Scottish aristocracy whose estate was not far away. Hamilton was a wing commander in the Royal Air Force at the time and, after meeting Hess, who revealed his true identity to him, informed the British prime minister, Winston Churchill, what had taken place. On being told, Churchill, who often relaxed by watching Hollywood films, is said to have remarked, "Hess or no Hess, I'm going to watch the Marx Brothers."

A PEACE SETTLEMENT

Hess joined the Nazi Party at its inception in 1920 and would have a fundamental influence on its direction. He had studied geopolitics under Professor Karl Haushofer at the University of Munich and introduced Hitler to the concept of *Lebensraum*, literally "living space," which became one of the cornerstones of Nazi ideology. The idea justified the need for German expansion in the east in order for the country to grow and prosper, and was behind the *Generalplan Ost* (Master Plan for the East) in which the Slavic and Jewish inhabitants of the territories to the east of Germany would be subjugated and replaced by ethnic Germans. Hitler thought that Germany had lost the First World War because it had fought on two fronts, in the west as well as the east, and was determined not to make the same mistake himself. Before Operation Barbarossa, the invasion of Russia, was due to begin in June 1941, he appears to have wanted to reach a settlement with Britain which would bring the war in the west to an end, allowing him to concentrate his forces on his main objective in the east.

Above: Rudolf Hess in 1933, when he became deputy Führer to Adolf Hitler. By 1941 his influence in the Nazi Party had declined.

The Battle of Britain, fought in the summer of 1940, was intended to drag Britain to the negotiating table with the threat of invasion, but the success of the RAF had forced Hitler to rethink his strategy. By that time, Hess had become less influential within the Nazi Party, his role as Hitler's right-hand man having largely been taken over by Martin Bormann. Hess appears to have been given the task of finding another way of reaching a settlement with Britain and, as it was thought that Churchill would never agree to negotiations, this would have to involve a plan which removed Churchill from power.

Left: Hitler and Hess, seen here in 1932, had been close friends. By flying to Scotland, Hess could have been trying to impress the Führer.

THE PEACE PARTY

While we don't know for certain what motivated Hess to fly to Scotland, it could have been part of his plan to achieve these aims by making contact with people in Britain who could lead an attempt to oust Churchill from the office of prime minister and then begin negotiations with Hitler. He appears to have convinced himself of the existence of a "peace party" in Britain, made up of Nazi sympathizers and politicians such as Neville Chamberlain and Lord Halifax, who had advocated appeasement before the start of the war, and he may have flown to Scotland because he thought the Duke of Hamilton was part of this group.

Hamilton had attended the Berlin Olympic Games in 1936 as part of a delegation invited by the German government, and there, had met a number of prominent Nazi officials. He would later say that he had not met Hess, but he is known to have attended at least one function at which the deputy führer was present. After Hess had been captured in Scotland, unsubstantiated rumors appeared in the press alleging that the Duke had been in contact with Hess before the flight, but nothing has come to light since to indicate that this was the case. Hess apparently chose Hamilton on the suggestion of Albrecht Haushofer, the son of Professor Karl Haushofer, who had met the duke in 1936 in Berlin. Whatever the case, no evidence exists to show that Hamilton was part of a peace party or, in fact, that any such organization existed at all.

One theory about the flight suggests that Hess was delivering detailed peace proposals from Hitler to the British government which made the offer of a German withdrawal from Western Europe in exchange for Britain giving Germany a free hand in the east. Hitler's reaction on being informed of what Hess had done was reported to be one of shock, in which he branded Hess a traitor to Germany who would be shot on sight if he ever returned. Such a reaction may have been staged after it had become clear that Hess's mission had failed, but it would appear more likely that Hess had acted alone, either against Hitler's wishes or without his knowledge. Having being sidelined by Bormann in the Nazi hierarchy, Hess may have been attempting to recover his position by pulling off a spectacular mission on his

Right: Spandau Prison in Berlin. Hess was held here from 1947 until his death in 1987, after which the building was demolished.

Above: Hess with Professor Karl Haushofer, an advocate of the concept of *Lebensraum*, which would become a key part of Nazi ideology.

own initiative to bring Britain to the negotiating table.

Once Hess had been taken into captivity, the British showed no sign of being interested in negotiating with him. He was held in prison until the end of the war and then sent back to Germany to face charges of war crimes at the Nuremberg trials. He was found guilty of crimes against peace and sentenced to life imprisonment. He was held in Spandau Prison until 1987, when, at the age of ninety-three, he committed suicide, hanging himself with an extension cord to a reading lamp. A number of conspiracy theories developed about Hess while he was in prison, most famously that the man captured in Scotland was not Hess at all but an imposter, and that he did not commit suicide but was murdered by the British, though no evidence has ever come to light to support either of these theories.

In typical fashion, the British government has not declassified all of the files it holds relating to Hess, even long after there can be any reason for them to remain secret, providing fuel to the conspiracy theorists and preventing historians from examining the Hess affair as fully as might otherwise be possible. Even if the files become available, we may never know for certain exactly what motivated Hess or what he had been hoping to achieve by flying to Scotland in the middle of the Second World War, leaving the affair to continue as a strange and unsolved enigma, much as Hess himself appears to have been.

— ALTERNATIVE —
THEORIES

According to secret British files released in 2004, a woman named as Mrs. Violet Roberts, the widow of a Cambridge University academic, wrote to Professor Karl Haushofer in Munich in 1940 via a post office box she had set up in Lisbon, in neutral Portugal. She expressed her regret that the war had interrupted their friendship and provided the number of the post office box for a reply. Professor Haushofer passed the letter on to his son, Albrecht, who made Hess aware of it. Albrecht Haushofer wrote back to Mrs. Roberts via Lisbon and enclosed a message which he asked her to pass on to the Duke of Hamilton, inviting him to a secret meeting in Lisbon.

Haushofer's reply was intercepted by MI5 and the message was not passed on to the duke for five months, opening up the possibility that, in the meantime, MI5 had entered into a correspondence with Hess through Haushofer by claiming to be the duke. This remains entirely speculative, but, if this was the

Above: Karl and Martha Haushofer with their two sons. Albrecht (left) attended his father's geopolitics classes together with Hess.

case, then could MI5 have lured Hess to Britain by making him think that the duke really was involved with a peace party and, by flying to Scotland himself, he would be entering into negotiations with senior British politicians? It may appear an unlikely scenario, but, then again, as so many aspects of the affair remain unexplained, it cannot be entirely discounted either.

WAS BRITISH PRIME MINISTER HAROLD WILSON A SOVIET SPY?

Date: 1963
Location: Britain

The prospect of a British prime minister being a KGB agent may sound ludicrous, but that was exactly what was alleged by a Soviet defector in 1963.

Harold Wilson first became a member of parliament for the Labour Party in the landslide 1945 election victory won by his party after the end of the Second World War. He was given a junior position in the Ministry of Works and in that capacity he traveled to the Soviet Union on a number of occasions as part of British trade delegations. During these trips he made a number of important contacts, including the Soviet foreign minister, Vyacheslav Molotov, and the minister of foreign trade, Anastas Mikoyan. He would stay in touch with both for a number of years afterward. Such contact between politicians of different countries was hardly unusual, particularly considering that Britain and the Soviet Union had been allies during the war, but it would come to assume greater significance after allegations were made that, during his trips to the Soviet Union, Wilson had been recruited by the KGB.

SOVIET CONTACTS

In January 1963, Hugh Gaitskell, the leader of the Labour Party during a long period of opposition, died suddenly at the age of fifty-six of complications arising from the autoimmune disease lupus. He was succeeded by Wilson, who became prime minister in the following year after Labour won the next general election. He would remain as prime minister for the next six years and then serve

Above: Harold Wilson, British prime minister from 1964 to 1970 and from 1974 to 1976, was accused of being a traitor to his country.

in that position again between 1974 and 1976, at which point he decided to step down. After leaving frontline politics, Wilson alleged that conservative elements within the British secret services had been conspiring against him for much of the time he had been prime minister. It would later emerge that MI5 had kept a file on him since 1945 and in 1963 had placed bugs within 10 Downing Street, the official residence of the prime minister, which had remained in place until 1977.

It would later be claimed that MI5 had placed the bugs because of the Profumo affair, in which John Profumo, the secretary of state for war, had lied to parliament about his relationship with the nineteen-year-old model Christine Keeler. Keeler, it emerged, had simultaneously been involved with a naval attaché from the Soviet embassy. However, the affair had occurred two years before the bugs were installed. An alternative reason could have been that, troubled by rumors which questioned Wilson's loyalties, MI5 was concerned about the possibility of him winning the 1964 general election. By 1963, MI5 had also been passed intelligence about Wilson obtained by the CIA from Anatoliy Golitsyn, who made the allegations of Wilson's KGB connections.

Above: Prime Minister
Harold Wilson (right)
meeting his Soviet
counterpart Alexei
Kosygin at Sheremetyevo
Airport, Moscow, in 1968.

GOLITSYN

Up until December 1961, Golitsyn had been a major in the KGB. He had been stationed in Helsinki, Finland, from where he defected to the United States. There he provided the CIA with details of a number of Soviet moles in the intelligence agencies of Western countries, including Kim Philby, one of the Cambridge spies who had been suspected by the British for some years (see page 210). With the net closing around him, Philby defected to the Soviet Union in January 1963, thus confirming that the information Golitsyn had given about him had been correct. In the circumstances, it is hardly surprising that MI5 would then take Golitsyn's allegations about Wilson seriously and begin an investigation into his activities. Golitsyn would go on to claim that Gaitskell had not died of natural causes, but had been assassinated by the KGB so that Wilson could become leader of the Labour Party.

Another defector who came to the West in 1992, after the collapse of the Soviet Union, shed some light on the murky world of the KGB's attempts to recruit agents and informers. Vasili Mitrokhin had been an archivist for the KGB since the 1940s and had made copies of thousands of documents, which he brought with him when he defected. Among this vast store were details of how information picked up by Wilson's Soviet contacts had been passed on to the KGB, where it was regarded as being valuable because it gave insights into the British government.

One file in the Mitrokhin archive provided details of KGB attempts to develop Wilson as an agent, but these apparently come

— ALTERNATIVE —
THEORIES

Beginning in 1973, MI5 and members of the British army in Northern Ireland are alleged to have begun a smear campaign known as Clockwork Orange, which attempted to discredit senior British politicians, in particular, Harold Wilson. This could have been the prelude to an attempted military coup to remove Wilson's government. On a number of occasions in 1974, the British Army mounted several anti-terrorist training exercises to occupy Heathrow Airport, and these have been described by some as being practice runs for the beginning of a coup. If this was the case, however, it did not progress beyond the training stage.

Above: British army tanks at Heathrow Airport in 1974 in an anti-terrorist training exercise. Could it really have been a practice run for a coup?

to nothing. As Wilson had held senior positions in the British government throughout his political career, he would have had access to top-secret and highly sensitive documents, but none of this material appears to have found its way to the KGB. As far as it is possible to tell, then, MI5 investigations into Wilson found no evidence that he had ever intentionally supplied the Soviet Union with secret intelligence. A faction within the service appears to have continued to suspect him nevertheless, which, as Wilson suspected, led to MI5 attempts to destabilize his governments.

WHY DID THE UK GOVERNMENT PROTECT THE IDENTITY OF ANTHONY BLUNT?

Date: 1964–1979
Location: UK

British intelligence uncovered the identity of the fourth man in the Cambridge spy ring in 1964, but kept it secret for fifteen years, a decision that is as yet unexplained.

All of the spies had been recruited to work for the Soviet Union at the University of Cambridge in the early 1930s. They had gone on to follow similar career paths from the university to the British Foreign Office, the diplomatic service, and, in some cases, the intelligence services during the Second World War. The ring began to unravel in 1951, when the United States decrypted Soviet diplomatic telegrams which pointed to the identity of one of the spies, Donald Maclean. He defected to the Soviet Union along with Guy Burgess before either of them could be arrested. As we saw previously, in 1961 the KGB defector Anatoliy Golitsyn identified the third man in the ring as Kim Philby, who also fled to the Soviet Union before being caught (see page 206). Golitsyn referred to the Cambridge spies as a "ring of five," leaving two more for the British intelligence services to find.

THE FOURTH MAN

The Cambridge connection between the three spies already unmasked was clear enough, and their known associates from that time now came under suspicion as being the fourth man in the spy ring. Anthony Blunt was a few years older than the others and had been a fellow of Trinity College rather than an undergraduate, as Burgess, Maclean, and Philby had been, but was one of their circle of friends. During the Second World War, he had worked for British intelligence at Bletchley Park, the country house in Buckinghamshire where British codebreakers cracked German Enigma ciphers. After the war, he did not pursue a career in intelligence, instead returning to academia as an art historian. In that capacity, he held a number of prestigious positions, including director of the Courtauld Institute of Art and Surveyor of the Queen's Pictures in the royal household, work for which he was awarded a knighthood.

Above: Anthony Blunt: as well as being a Soviet agent, Blunt was a respected art historian and Surveyor of the Queen's Pictures.

In 1964, Michael Straight, an American who had attended Trinity College, Cambridge, in the early 1930s, admitted that he had been recruited by the Soviet Union as a spy and named Blunt as the man who had recruited him. Straight came from a prominent and wealthy family, which provided him with the contacts to get a job in the U.S. State Department when he returned to the United States from Cambridge. He does not appear to have had access to any secret documents, but he did pass information to the KGB which provided intelligence on the workings of the U.S. government. In 1963, he was offered the post of chairman of the Advisory Council on the Arts by the Kennedy administration, and in the knowledge that this

Above: Four of the Cambridge spies—clockwise from top left: Anthony Blunt, Donald Maclean, Kim Philby, and Guy Burgess.

would require a security check, he confessed his involvement with the KGB to the FBI, revealing Blunt's identity in the process.

EXPOSED AND PROTECTED

Blunt was interrogated by MI5 in April 1964 and offered immunity from prosecution in exchange for a full confession. It is not clear why this offer was made, given that Straight had already provided details of Blunt's involvement with the KGB, even if this would have required corroborating evidence for a prosecution to have been brought against him. One possibility is that MI5 did not want to go through the embarrassment of having another Soviet mole publicly unmasked so soon after Philby had defected, but it is also possible that Blunt was in possession of information of some kind which he used as a bargaining chip to ensure that not only was he not prosecuted but his identity was protected.

One theory alleges that Blunt had obtained details of letters written by the Duke of Windsor during the Second World War to his German relative Philipp of Hesse, who, in common with the duke, was a great-grandson of Queen Victoria. Philipp had joined the Nazis in 1930, and had held a prominent position in the party until his arrest and imprisonment in 1943. It has been alleged that he could have acted as a secret conduit for messages between the duke and Adolf Hitler in the period following the duke's abdication from the British throne, in December 1936, up until August 1940, at which point he was appointed governor of the Bahamas, perhaps as a means of removing him from any further Nazi influence.

In August 1945, Blunt had been sent on a mission to Germany on behalf of the king, with the stated purpose of retrieving an archive of letters written by Queen Victoria to her eldest daughter, also called Victoria. She had married the German emperor Frederick III and after his death in 1888 had lived at Schloss Friedrichshof, near Frankfurt. The Queen's letters to her daughter were kept in the library at Friedrichshof and, after the U.S. Army commandeered the building at the end of the war, they were thought to be at risk of being stolen or destroyed.

It has been suggested that the retrieval of Queen Victoria's letters was a cover for the real purpose of Blunt's trip, which could have been to secure any surviving letters written by the Duke of Windsor to Philipp of Hesse showing that he really did hold Nazi sympathies and perhaps even colluded with Germany during the Second World War. If any such letters had fallen into the wrong hands and been published, it could have been extremely embarrassing for the British royal family, fueling rumors that the duke had consorted with the enemy during wartime and perhaps even committed treason.

No letters between the Duke of Windsor and Philipp of Hesse have ever come to light, but if such incriminating documents really did exist and had been found by Blunt then he could have used his knowledge of the contents as a bargaining chip once he had been exposed as a Soviet spy. In exchange for his continued silence on the matter, his identity as the fourth man in the Cambridge spy ring was protected by MI5. This remained the case until November

Below: Philipp of Hesse with his wife, Princess Mafalda. He was the great-grandson of Queen Victoria and joined the Nazi Party in 1930.

Left: Anthony Blunt vsisited Schloss Friedrichshof, now the Schlosshotel Kronberg, in 1945, ostensibly to retrieve letters written by Queen Victoria.

1979, when the journalist Andrew Boyle published *A Climate of Treason*, a book about the Cambridge spies which, while not actually naming Blunt as the fourth man, provided enough details for his identity to become apparent. Shortly afterward, the British prime minister, Margaret Thatcher, named Blunt in the House of Commons and he became the subject of intense media scrutiny. He died four years later, in 1983, at the age of seventy-five; if he really had come across any information in Schloss Friedrichshof which he had used to protect himself, then those secrets, whatever they may have been, appear to have died with him.

His continued silence in the period between his exposure and his death could be taken as an indication that he did not in fact posess any scandalous information which he could use as a bargaining chip, because he would have had no reason to continue to keep it secret. If this was the case, then there must surely have been another reason why the British government allowed a known Soviet spy to go unpunished for his acts of treason.

— ALTERNATIVE —
THEORIES

In his controversial book *Spycatcher*, published in 1987, the retired MI5 officer Peter Wright proposed a different explanation for the question of why Blunt had been offered immunity from prosecution. According to Wright, who had been involved in Blunt's interrogation, Roger Hollis, the director general of MI5 at the time, decided to offer Blunt immunity to prevent another scandal damaging the Conservative party in the run-up to the 1964 parliamentary elections. The Conservative government had already been severely embarrassed by the Profumo affair, the defection of Kim Philby, and the exposure in September 1962 of John Vassall, a civil servant working in the British Admiralty who had spied for the Soviet Union. If Blunt had been exposed, revelations about his activities would have caused further trouble for the Conservatives, particularly in light of his connection to the royal household.

Above: Roger Hollis, the director general of MI5 from 1953 to 1965, was accused by Peter Wright of being a Soviet mole.

Wright also alleged that Hollis was himself a Soviet mole, but does not explore the possibility that, if this was the case, then perhaps Hollis protected Blunt to prevent his own exposure or to stop him from naming other Soviet moles whose identities remained unknown to British intelligence. Debates continue concerning Blunt and Hollis, but we may never know the true story.

DID THE PAKISTANI INTELLIGENCE SERVICE SHELTER OSAMA BIN LADEN?

Date: 2001–2011
Location: Pakistan

It took the United States ten years to track down Osama bin Laden. Had the ISI, the Pakistani intelligence service, known where he was the whole time?

On the night of May 2, 2011, U.S. Special Forces launched a raid ordered by President Barack Obama on a compound near the city of Abbottabad in northeastern Pakistan. During the course of the operation, Osama bin Laden was shot dead by a Navy Seal and his body was taken away to be identified and then buried at sea. It was the culmination of a manhunt which had begun with the U.S.-led invasion of Afghanistan in October 2001, in the aftermath of the al-Qaeda terrorist attacks of 9/11 (see page 84). A number of different accounts exist concerning how bin Laden was found. In one, a Pakistani intelligence officer is said to have contacted the CIA to tell them where he was in order to collect the $25 million reward offered by the United States, while another suggests that information obtained from al-Qaeda prisoners at the Guantanamo

Bay detention camp in Cuba led the CIA to uncovering the identity of one of bin Laden's couriers, who was then located and followed to Abbottabad, to bin Laden's compound.

ISI INVOLVEMENT

The compound had been built during the course of 2005 and comprised a three-story house, a guesthouse, and a number

of smaller buildings surrounded by a high wall. It was situated less than a mile from Pakistan's principal military academy, and bin Laden is thought to have been living there with members of his family from early 2006, making it hard to believe that his location was not known in Pakistan and opening up the possibility that he was being protected. Rumors of ISI involvement with al-Qaeda had been circulating since the invasion of Afghanistan had forced the organization out of the country, and it is generally accepted that Pakistani agents facilitated the escape of al-Qaeda members across the border into the region of North Waziristan in Pakistan, from where they mounted raids against the Afghan government and Western forces in Afghanistan.

Above: The compound in Abbottabad, Pakistan, where Osama bin Laden lived with his family from 2006 until his death in 2011.

What has not been established is whether the ISI operatives involved were part of a rogue faction within the military and intelligence service which supported the Taliban and al-Qaeda, or if they were acting on orders from higher up. Unproven allegations have accused Pervez Musharraf, the president of Pakistan from 2001 to 2008, of at the very least knowing about the activities of the intelligence services, and have also claimed that, rather than bin Laden hiding in Pakistan, he had been provided with a safe house. A commission set up in Pakistan to investigate the circumstances of bin Laden's death did not support such

Ten Most Wanted

The FBI is offering rewards for information leading to the apprehension of the Ten Most Wanted Fugitives. Select the images of suspects to display more information.

Facts on the Program | Historical Photos of Each Top Tenner | 60th Anniversary Booklet

USAMA BIN LADEN

Murder of U.S. Nationals Outside the United States; Conspiracy to Murder U.S. Nationals Outside the United States; Attack on a Federal Facility Resulting in D...

REWARD: The Rewards For Justice Program, United States Department of State, is offering a reward of up to $25 million for information leading directly to the apprehension or conviction of Usama Bin Laden. An additional $2 million is being offered through a program developed and funded by the Airline Pilots Association and the Air Transport Association.

Usama Bin Laden is wanted in connection with the August 7, 1998, bombings of the United States Embassies in Dar es Salaam, Tanzania, and Nairobi, Kenya. These attacks killed over 200 people. In addition, Bin Laden is a suspect in other terrorist attacks throughout the world.

Bin Laden is the leader of a terrorist organization known as Al-Qaeda, "The Base". He is left-handed and walks with a cane.

Above: The FBI's Ten Most Wanted webpage from May 3, 2011, the day after the Abbottabad raid. Osama bin Laden is listed as "deceased."

allegations, instead finding that bin Laden had been able to live in Pakistan for more than nine years after fleeing from Afghanistan because of gross incompetence and negligence within the government, military, and intelligence service. The report did not rule out the possible collusion of some ISI officers in shielding bin Laden, but did not find any direct evidence and could not link any such actions to a wider conspiracy.

A BIGGER PICTURE

The investigative journalist Seymour Hersh has disputed almost every aspect of the official account of the U.S. operation against bin Laden, including the role played by the Pakistani government and the ISI. According to his sources, bin Laden had been captured by ISI agents sometime around 2006 and was being held under guard in what amounted to house arrest in Abbottabad. When it suited the Pakistani government, they informed the United States and President Obama then ordered the raid at a moment of his choosing. According to Hersh, May 2011 was the best time for Obama because an operation to kill bin Laden at that moment would have the effect of increasing his popularity among the American electorate—perfect timing for the presidential election scheduled to take place eighteen months later, which he won with a comfortable majority.

The official account of the raid states that the Americans did not warn the Pakistani authorities in advance because of fears of security leaks, but Hersh has alleged that this was not the case. According to his version of events, the Pakistani military were

— ALTERNATIVE —
THEORIES

Pakistan supported the Taliban regime in Afghanistan because they both opposed India's growing influence in the region. The Taliban sheltered al-Qaeda until being ousted by the 2001 invasion, and the new Afghan government began to develop friendly relations with India, which could explain why the Pakistani government tolerated the presence of Taliban and al-Qaeda fighters in Pakistan, and allowed them to mount attacks across the border. Protecting bin Laden could have been part of this policy of opposing Indian influence, but when the Taliban began attacks within Pakistan, the government

Above: A Pakistani army operation against Taliban insurgents in 2009. The insurgency may have led Pakistan to stop protecting bin Laden.

may have decided that bin Laden had become a liability and so given him up to the Americans.

well aware of the planned raid and allowed it to happen without interference, either because they had decided to stop protecting bin Laden or because they wanted to curry favor with the United States. Hersh has not revealed the source of his information so it is impossible to verify the story, which has been vigorously denied in the United States and Pakistan. Essentially, though, he is saying that bin Laden's whereabouts had been known for some time to the United States as well as to Pakistan, and the two countries colluded with each other so that he could be killed at a time which best suited both governments.

FURTHER READING

BOOKS

Aaronovitch, David. *Voodoo Histories: The Role of the Conspiracy Theory in Shaping Modern History*. London: Jonathan Cape, 2009.

Akçam, Taner. *A Shameful Act: The Armenian Genocide and the Question of Turkish Responsibility*. London: Constable, 2007.

Andrew, Christopher. *The Defence of the Realm: The Authorized History of MI5*. London: Allen Lane, 2009.

Bloch, Michael. *Operation Willi: The Plot to Kidnap the Duke of Windsor, July 1940*. London: Weidenfeld and Nicolson, 1984.

Brotherton, Rob. *Suspicious Minds: Why We Believe Conspiracy Theories*. London: Bloomsbury, 2016.

Carter, Miranda. *Anthony Blunt: His Lives*. London: Pan, 2001.

Clark, Christopher. *The Sleepwalkers: How Europe Went to War in 1914*. London: Allen Lane, 2012.

Cohn, Norman. *Warrant for Genocide: The Myth of the Jewish World-conspiracy and the Protocols of the Elders of Zion*. London: Eyre and Spottiswoode, 1966.

Dudgeon, Jeffrey. *Roger Casement: The Black Diaries*. Belfast: Belfast Press, 2016.

Emery, Fred. *Watergate: The Corruption of American Politics and the Fall of Richard Nixon*. New York: Touchstone, 1994.

Harding, Luke: *A Very Expensive Poison: The Definitive Story of the Murder of Litvinenko and Russia's War with the West*. London: Guardian Faber Publishing, 2016.

Hett, Benjamin Carter. *Burning the Reichstag: An Investigation into the Third Reich's Enduring Mystery*. Oxford: Oxford University Press, 2014.

Jones, Owen. *The Establishment: And How They Get Away With It*. London: Penguin, 2015.

Kaiser, David. *The Road to Dallas: The Assassination of John F. Kennedy*. Cambridge, MA: Harvard University Press, 2008.

Prange, Gordon W. *At Dawn We Slept: The Untold Story of Pearl Harbor*. London: Michael Joseph, 1982.

Stafford, David, ed. *Flight from Reality: Rudolf Hess and His Mission to Scotland 1941*. London: Pimlico, 2002.

Steinacher, Gerald. *Nazis on the Run: How Hitler's Henchmen Fled Justice*. Oxford: Oxford University Press, 2011.

Tyldesley, Joyce. *Tutankhamen's Curse: The Developing History of an Egyptian King*. London: Profile Books, 2012.

Williams, Susan. *Who Killed Hammarskjöld? The UN, the Cold War and White Supremacy in Africa*. London: Hurst Publishers, 2011.

Wright, Peter. *Spycatcher: The Candid Autobiography of a Senior Intelligence Officer*. London: Viking, 1987.

WEBSITES

Bilderberg Meetings: The Official Website
bilderbergmeetings.org

Conspiracies.net
conspiracies.net

"Debunking the 9/11 Myths: Special Report: The World Trade Center"
popularmechanics.com/military/a6384/debunking-911-myths-world-trade-center

RationalWiki
rationalwiki.org

Taken for a Ride (a PBS documentary on the decline of the streetcar)
pbs.org/pov/takenforaride

"The Unbelievable Tale of Jesus' Wife"
theatlantic.com/magazine/archive/2016/07/the-unbelievable-tale-of-jesus-wife/485573/

Understanding the Iran-Contra Affairs
brown.edu/Research/Understanding_the_Iran_Contra_Affair

The Vatican Secret Archive
archiviosegretovaticano.va/content/archiviosegretovaticano/en.html

WikiLeaks
wikileaks.org

INDEX

IMAGE CREDITS

Cover: © Symonenko Viktoriia | Shutterstock
7: © Zvonimir Atletic | Shutterstock
12: © Jeff Dahl | Creative Commons
13: © Carsten Frenzl | Creative Commons
14: © Dmitry Denisenkov | Creative Commons
15: © Pataki Márta | Creative Commons
19: © nishioka1987 | Shutterstock
27, 71, 72, 157: © Everett Historical | Shutterstock
32, 49: © Associated Press
34: © MPI | Getty Images
35: © Patrick Gruban | Creative Commons
40, 209: © Bettmann | Getty Images
45: © Pierre Boussel | Getty Images
46: © Bobak Ha'Eri | Creative Commons
47: © amer ghazzal | Alamy Stock Photo
50: © Sadik Gulec | Shutterstock
51: © Jenny Matthews | Alamy Stock Photo
53: © Gilles BASSIGNAC | Getty Images
55: © Photo 12 | Alamy Stock Photo
57: © Petar Jevtic | Shutterstock
58, 85: © 9/11 Photos | Creative Commons
61: © Musee des Beaux-Arts Andre Malraux,
      Le Havre | Bridgeman Images
63: © salajean | Shutterstock
69: © Tim Evanson | Creative Commons
78: © National Cryptologic Museum, NSA
83: © mark reinstein | Shutterstock
86: © TheMachineStops (Robert J. Fisch) | Creative Commons
94: © Vibrant Pictures | Alamy Stock Photo
103: © Andrey_Kuzmin | Shutterstock
105: © Metro Library and Archive
106: © Retrograph Collection | Mary Evans

110, 172: © Everett Collection | Mary Evans
111: © Everett Collection | Alamy Stock Photo
115, 150: © Universal History Archive | Getty Images
127: © Tiamonol Creative Commons
131: © Couperfield | Shutterstock
133: © Barnara Alper | Getty Images
139: © World Imaging | Creative Commons
141: © BeBa | Iberfoto | Mary Evans
143: © Shane Global | Creative Commons
155, 165: © Mary Evans
159, 200: © Sueddeutsche Zeitung Photo | Mary Evans
164: © Urban | Creative Commons
167: © Henk Monster | Creative Commons
168: © Gage Skidmore | Creative Commons
169: © Shepherd Johnson | Creative Commons
174: © Kenneth Lu | Creative Commons
175: © Sarah Stierch | Creative Commons
176: © Rolls Press | Popperfoto | Getty Images
185: © Illustrated London News Ltd | Mary Evans
186: © McMahon | Getty Images
187: © Topical Press Agency | Getty Images
193: © Weimar Archive | Mary Evans
197: © Pharcide | Mary Evans
199: © Bundesarchiv, Bild 146II-849 | Creative Commons
201: © Bauamt Süd, Einofski | Creative Commons
203: © Henry Guttmann | Getty Images
205: © Allen Warren | Creative Commons
206: © Central Press | Getty Images
207: © Keystone Pictures USA | Alamy
210, 213: © Keystone | Getty Images
213: © dontworry | Creative Commons
215: © Sajjad Ali Qureshi | Creative Commons
217: © Al Jazeera English | Creative Commons